MINI MEATBALLS STUFFED WITH ROASTED PISTACHIOS
SEE PAGE 58

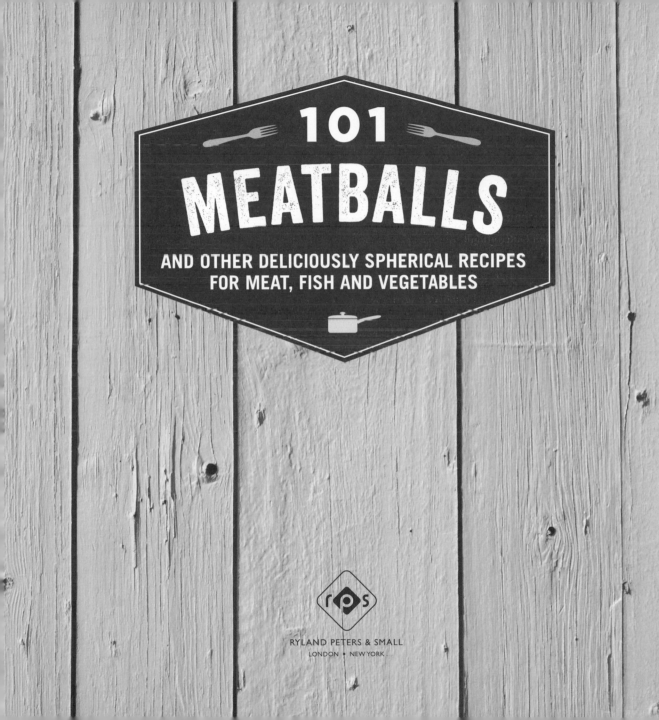

101
MEATBALLS

AND OTHER DELICIOUSLY SPHERICAL RECIPES FOR MEAT, FISH AND VEGETABLES

RYLAND PETERS & SMALL
LONDON • NEW YORK

First published in 2016 by
Ryland Peters & Small
20–21 Jockey's Fields
London WC1R 4BW
and

341 E 116th St
New York, NY 10029
www.rylandpeters.com

Recipe collection compiled
by Alice Sambrook. Recipe text ©
Annie Rigg, Belinda Williams, Brian
Glover, Brontë Aurell, Carol Hilker,
Cathy Seward, Chloe Coker, Clare
Ferguson, Dan May, Dunja Gulin,
Ghillie Basan, Jackie Kearney, Jane
Montgomery, Jenny Linford, Jordan
Bourke, Julz Beresford, Laura
Washburn, Linda Collister, Liz
Franklin, Louise Pickford, Lydia
France, Maxine Clark, Milli Taylor,
Miranda Ballard, Rachael Anne Hill,
Rena Salaman, Ross Dobson, Silvana
Franco, Sonia Stevenson, Sunil
Vijayakar, Tonia George, Tori
Haschka, Tori Finch, Uyen Luu,
Valerie Aikman-Smith, Vatcharin
Bhumichitr, Vicky Jones and Ryland
Peters & Small.

Design & photography
© Ryland Peters & Small 2016

A CIP catalog record for this book is
available from the Library of
Congress and the British Library.

ISBN: 978-1-84975-774-4

Printed in China

10 9 8 7 6 5 4 3 2 1

Editors: Alice Sambrook
Designer: Paul Stradling
Production: David Hearn
Editorial Director: Julia Charles
Art Director: Leslie Harrington
Publisher: Cindy Richards
Indexer: Vanessa Bird

NOTES

• Some cheeses such as Parmesan are
made using animal rennet and are
therefore not suitable for strict
vegetarians. It can depend on the
brand so always check the label first
and use a vegetarian substitute where
required.

• Both British (metric) and American
(imperial plus US cups) are included;
however, its important not to alternate
between the two within a recipe.

• All eggs are medium (UK)
or large (US), unless otherwise
specified. It is recommended
that free-range, organic eggs
be used whenever possible. Recipes
containing raw or partially cooked
egg should not be served to the very
young, very old, anyone with
a compromised immune
system or pregnant women.

• When a recipe calls for
grated zest of citrus fruit, buy
unwaxed fruit and wash well before
use. If you can only find treated fruit,
scrub and rinse before using.

• Ovens should be preheated to the
specified temperatures. All ovens work
slightly differently. We recommend
using an oven thermometer and
suggest you consult the maker's
handbook for any special instructions,
particularly if you are cooking in a
fan-assisted/convection oven, as you
may need to adjust temperatures.

CONTENTS

INTRODUCTION

MEATBALLS ARE A DISH SO WELL-LOVED THAT EACH COUNTRY HAS THEIR OWN SPECIALITY AND EACH FAMILY HAS A FAVOURITE RECIPE, OFTEN HANDED DOWN THROUGH GENERATIONS, WHETHER AN ITALIAN *NONA* WHO MADE THE BEST *POLPETTE* OR A SPANISH *ABUELA* WITH A SECRET RECIPE FOR OUTSTANDING *ALBONDIGAS*. HERE ARE SOME HANDY HINTS AND TIPS ON CREATING THE BEST BALLS POSSIBLE, BUT REMEMBER THIS IS ONLY A ROUGH GUIDE – REALLY ANYONE CAN MAKE DELICIOUS MEATBALLS.

THE MEAT: There is something so satisfying about moulding together your favourite food and flavourings into a perfect little bite-sized ball. The wonderful thing about meatballs is that so many different things can work as the base. The defining feature need not be the nature of the 'meat', but the way that a creative blend of spices and herbs can be combined and rolled together to create a perfect mouthful. When choosing meat, bear in mind that a higher fat content often leads to a softer ball. So a high-fat minced pork will probably be softer in texture than a lean ground turkey meatball. If you are not a meat eater, so what?! Vegetables, pulses, grains, cheeses and fish make some of the tastiest balls in this book. Risotto, mashed chickpeas and potato are particularly nice: easy to mould and great carriers for plenty of herbs and spices.

THE MAGIC: The magic comes from what is added to the base 'meat' mixture. Garlic, onions, herbs, spices and breadcrumbs are all favourites. Don't be scared to play around with different combinations, rarely will a mixture of herbs and spices taste awful in a meatball unless you *really* overload on one thing. Wet ingredients like soy sauce, honey Worcestershire sauce, or flavoured oils can be great additions, just remember they will change the texture. You can always fix an overly wet mixture by adding a little flour or breadcrumbs and an overly dry mixture by adding milk, oil or an egg.

THE MAKING: Always use damp or lightly oiled hands with a sticky mixture, otherwise you might end up washing most of it down the sink. Try not to pack the balls too tightly or overmix the meat – both these things can result in a tough meatball. Be firm but gentle, and though it may be messy, using your hands is really the only way to be able to properly tell when everything is just combined. Refrigerating balls before cooking can help them to firm up and keep their shape, this is also useful if you want to make them the day before cooking.

CHAPTER 1
BEEF

500 g/1 lb. 2 oz. dried spaghetti

salt, to taste

spaghetti sauce

90 g/¾ cup chopped onion

6 garlic cloves, crushed

50 g/¼ cup extra virgin olive oil

2 x 400 g/14-oz. cans whole, peeled tomatoes

2 teaspoons sea salt

1 teaspoon caster/granulated sugar

1 fresh bay leaf

170 g/6 oz. tomato purée/paste

¾ teaspoon dried basil

½ teaspoon ground black pepper

meatballs

2 tablespoons extra virgin olive oil

225 g/8 oz. lean minced/ground beef

225 g/8 oz. ground thin/short rib

60 g/1 cup fresh breadcrumbs

1 tablespoon dried parsley

2 tablespoons Parmesan cheese, grated, plus extra for sprinkling

¼ teaspoon ground black pepper

a pinch of garlic powder

1 egg, beaten

serves 4

CLASSIC SPAGHETTI & MEATBALLS

THIS HEARTY AND SATISFYING RECIPE IS ONE THAT WILL BE REQUESTED TIME AND TIME AGAIN BY FRIENDS AND FAMILY MEMBERS, AND PASSED DOWN THROUGH GENERATIONS. TO GIVE AN EXTRA-RICH FLAVOUR YOU CAN ALSO MAKE THIS DISH IN A SLOW COOKER.

★ For the spaghetti sauce, in a large saucepan over a medium heat, sauté the onion and garlic in the olive oil until the onion is translucent. Stir in the tomatoes, salt, sugar and bay leaf. Cover the saucepan and reduce the heat to low. Simmer for 1–1½ hours. Stir in the tomato purée/paste, basil and black pepper. Refrigerate until ready to use.

★ Preheat the oven to 190°C (375°F) Gas 5.

★ For the meatballs, combine all the ingredients well in a mixing bowl using damp hands and form into golf-ball-sized balls. Put on a baking sheet and transfer to the preheated oven for 20 minutes. Use immediately or turn out onto a plate to cool and then place in the freezer.

★ Bring a pot of salted water to the boil and add the pasta. When the pasta reaches an al dente texture, about 8–10 minutes, remove and drain. Mix with the sauce, add the meatballs and finish by adding a generous sprinkling of freshly grated Parmesan cheese.

★ To make in a slow-cooker, set the heat to its lowest setting and cook the meatballs and sauce for 6–8 hours. Follow the above directions for cooking the pasta.

3 tablespoons olive oil

2 onions, finely chopped

3 large garlic cloves, crushed

1 teaspoon dried oregano

½ teaspoon hot red pepper flakes

½ teaspoon ground cumin

200 ml/¾ cup red wine

400-g/14-oz. can chopped tomatoes

1 strip of orange peel

1 teaspoon caster/granulated sugar

sea salt and freshly ground black pepper

albóndigas

200 g/6½ oz. good-quality pork sausages

350 g/12 oz. lean minced/ground beef

1 teaspoon Spanish smoked paprika

½ teaspoon ground cumin

2 generous tablespoons freshly chopped flat-leaf parsley, plus extra to garnish

1 small egg, beaten

3 tablespoons fresh breadcrumbs

1 tablespoon whole milk

serves 4–6

SPANISH *ALBÓNDIGAS*

YOU CAN PREPARE THESE FLAVOURFUL MEATBALLS AND THEIR SPICED TOMATO SAUCE AHEAD AND REHEAT IN A COVERED CASSEROLE DISH EITHER IN A MODERATE OVEN OR ON THE STOVETOP. THE TASTE REALLY INTENSIFIES IF YOU MAKE THEM A DAY OR SO IN ADVANCE.

★ Heat 2 tablespoons of the oil in a frying pan/skillet and fry the onions until soft but not coloured. Add the garlic and oregano and continue to cook for 1 minute. Scoop half the onions into a bowl and let cool.

★ Add the hot red pepper flakes and ground cumin to the pan/skillet and cook for 30 seconds. Add the red wine, chopped tomatoes and orange peel and cook gently for about 30 minutes, or until the sauce has thickened slightly. Add the sugar and season well with salt and pepper to balance the flavours. Remove from the heat and set aside while you prepare the albóndigas.

★ To make the albóndigas, remove the skin from the sausages and add the meat to the cooked onions along with the beef, paprika, ground cumin, parsley, egg, breadcrumbs and milk. Season well with salt and pepper. Using damp hands, mix well to combine and shape into 20 walnut-sized balls.

★ Heat the remaining oil in a large frying pan/skillet and brown the albóndigas in batches, adding more oil if necessary.

★ Add the albóndigas to the spiced tomato sauce and cook gently over a low heat for a further 30 minutes. Sprinkle more chopped parsley over the top before serving.

ITALIAN *POLPETTE*

POLPETTE OR ITALIAN MEATBALLS TYPICALLY USE A LARGE
QUANTITY OF FRESH WHITE BREADCRUMBS. THIS IS BY NO MEANS A
DECISION SOLELY MOTIVATED BY THRIFTINESS, THOUGH. IT HAS THE
EFFECT OF LIGHTENING THE MEATBALLS, WHICH ABSORB MUCH
MORE OF THE SAUCE AND FLAVOURSOME OIL RELEASED BY THE
MEAT. A SIMPLE TOMATO SAUCE IS ALL THAT'S NEEDED TO
ACCOMPANY, AS THE MEATBALLS REALLY ARE THE STAR OF THE
SHOW. ADD TO THIS MEAL A GLASS OF CHIANTI AND A BOX SET OF
THE SOPRANOS: NOW THAT'S A GOOD SUNDAY NIGHT IN.

★ To make the tomato sauce, put the olive oil, garlic, onion, tomatoes and
basil in a saucepan, season well and bring to the boil. Reduce the heat and
simmer gently for at least 40 minutes while you prepare the meatballs.

★ Preheat the oven to 200°C (400°F) Gas 6.

★ To make the meatballs, put the beef, breadcrumbs, eggs, Parmesan
cheese, parsley and olive oil in a large mixing bowl and season. Using
damp hands, mix well to combine and shape into roughly 20 walnut-sized
balls. Put them in a single layer on a baking sheet covered with foil.
Roast for 10 minutes in the preheated oven, turn, and continue to roast for
a further 6–7 minutes.

★ Cook the spaghetti in a saucepan of boiling salted water for 8–10
minutes until al dente. Drain, return to the pan and add the tomato sauce
and meatballs. Stir very gently so as not to break up the meatballs. Take
out the onion wedges if you prefer. Transfer to bowls and sprinkle with
basil and grated Parmesan cheese.

300–400 g/10½–14 oz. dried
spaghetti

sea salt and freshly ground black
pepper

tomato sauce

4 tablespoons extra virgin olive oil

3 garlic cloves, thinly sliced

1 large onion, cut into wedges

2 x 400-g/14-oz. cans chopped
tomatoes

20 g/¾ cup fresh basil, plus extra to
serve

meatballs

250 g/9 oz. minced/ground beef

100 g/1¾ cups fresh breadcrumbs

2 eggs

25 g/⅓ cup freshly grated Parmesan
cheese, plus extra to serve

4 tablespoons freshly chopped flat-
leaf parsley

3 tablespoons extra virgin olive oil

serves 4

SWEDISH MEATBALLS

30 g/⅓ cup porridge/old-fashioned oats or breadcrumbs

150 ml/⅔ cup beef or chicken stock

400 g/14 oz. minced/ground beef

250 g/9 oz. minced/ground pork (minimum 10% fat)

1 egg

2½ tablespoons plain/all-purpose flour

a pinch of salt

1 teaspoon ground allspice

½ teaspoon ground black pepper

½ teaspoon ground white pepper

a dash of Worcestershire sauce or soy sauce

1 small onion, grated/minced

butter and oil, for frying

mashed potato, to serve

lingonberries

250 g/9 oz. frozen lingonberries (available in some speciality food stores and online)

100 g/½ cup caster/granulated sugar

cream gravy

meat stock

1 tablespoon plain/all-purpose flour

a good glug of single/light cream

salt and freshly ground black pepper

serves 6

THERE ARE AS MANY RECIPES FOR MEATBALLS IN SCANDINAVIA AS THERE ARE COOKS, THOUGH THE SWEDISH VERSION IS ARGUABLY THE MOST FAMOUS. THE CLASSIC ACCOMPANIMENT OF A RICH GRAVY, CREAMY MASH AND TANGY LINGONBERRIES IS SUBLIME.

★ If using oats, soak them in the beef or chicken stock for 5 minutes. Mix the minced/ground meat with a good pinch of salt for a couple of minutes in a food processor to blend thoroughly. In another bowl, mix the eggs, flour, spices and Worcestershire or soy sauce with the soaked oats or breadcrumbs and grated/minced onion, then add this to the meat mixture. Leave this to rest for 20–25 minutes before using.

★ Heat a small knob/pat of butter or oil in a frying pan/skillet and, using damp hands, shape one small meatball and fry until cooked. Taste and adjust the seasoning. Continue to shape the mixture, using damp hands, into meatballs around 2.5 cm/1 inch in diameter, or larger if desired.

★ Melt a knob/pat of butter in a frying pan/skillet with a dash of oil and carefully add a few meatballs – make sure there is plenty of room to turn them so they get a uniform round shape and don't stick. Cook in batches for around 5 minutes at a time. Keep in a warm oven until needed.

★ When your meatballs are done, keep the pan on a medium heat. Add a tablespoon of flour to the fat in the pan (adding more butter if needed) and whisk, then add a splash of stock and whisk again as you bring to the boil. Keep adding stock until you have a creamy gravy, then add a good dollop of single/light cream and season with salt and pepper.

★ For the lingonberries, add the caster/granulated sugar and stir until the sugar dissolves and the berries have defrosted. Serve with the meatballs, mashed potatoes and gravy. Store leftover lingonberries in the fridge.

SPICY INDIAN GARLIC MEATBALLS

500 g/1 lb. 2 oz. minced/ground beef

1 garlic clove, crushed with a pinch of salt

1 teaspoon ground cumin

2 teaspoons ground coriander

2 tablespoons sunflower or vegetable oil

1 onion, finely chopped

1 garlic clove, chopped

2-cm/¾-inch piece fresh ginger, finely chopped

1 cinnamon stick

4 cardamom pods

a handful of fresh or frozen (not dried) curry leaves (optional)

400-g/14-oz. can chopped tomatoes

¼ teaspoon ground turmeric

¼ teaspoon chilli powder/hot red pepper powder (optional)

salt and freshly ground black pepper

torn fresh coriander/cilantro leaves, to garnish

serves 4

MINCED/GROUND BEEF DOESN'T HAVE TO BE DULL, AS THIS RECIPE PROVES WITH ITS ARRAY OF SPICES. SERVE THESE MEATBALLS WITH RICE AND A VEGETABLE SIDE DISH.

★ First, make the meatballs. Mix together the beef, crushed garlic, cumin and coriander and season well with salt and pepper. Using damp hands, shape the mixture into small meatballs, each roughly the size of a large marble.

★ Heat 1 tablespoon of the oil in a large, lidded frying pan/skillet and fry the meatballs until browned on all sides. Set aside.

★ Add the remaining oil to the pan. Fry the onion, garlic, ginger, cinnamon stick and cardamom pods, stirring, until the onion has softened. Mix in the curry leaves, if using, frying briefly, then add the chopped tomatoes. Add in the turmeric, chilli/hot red pepper powder and 300 ml/1¼ cups water. Season with salt. Bring to the boil.

★ Add the browned meatballs, bring to the boil once more, then cover, reduce the heat and cook for 15 minutes, stirring now and then. Uncover and cook for a further 10 minutes, stirring often, until the sauce has reduced and thickened. Serve at once, garnished with the fresh coriander/cilantro.

MEATBALL TAGINE

½ onion, coarsely chopped

a few sprigs of fresh flat-leaf parsley

a few sprigs of fresh coriander/cilantro

500 g/1 lb. 2 oz. minced/ground beef

1½ teaspoons sea salt

½ teaspoon ground white pepper

1 teaspoon ground cumin

1 teaspoon paprika

1 tablespoon fresh breadcrumbs

4 eggs, to serve (optional)

spicy tomato sauce

1½ onions

a small handful of fresh flat-leaf parsley

2 garlic cloves

400-g/14-oz. can chopped tomatoes

300 ml/1¼ cups stock (chicken, lamb or vegetable) or water

1½ teaspoons ground cumin

1 teaspoon ground white pepper

¼ teaspoon ground cinnamon

¼–½ teaspoon cayenne pepper, according to taste

a pinch of caster/granulated sugar

serves 4

THIS IS AN UNUSUAL BUT AUTHENTIC MOROCCAN RECIPE. TRADITIONALLY PREPARED IN A TAGINE, THE EGGS ARE COOKED IN THE DISH WITH THE MEATBALLS, ON TOP OF THE SAUCE. HOWEVER, THIS RECIPE COOKS THE EGGS SEPARATELY, ALLOWING FOR PREPARATION IN A FRYING PAN/SKILLET.

★ To make the meatballs, put the chopped onion in a food processor with the parsley and coriander/cilantro. Process until finely chopped. Add the beef and use the pulse button to obtain a smooth paste. Transfer to a bowl.

★ Add the salt, pepper, cumin, paprika and breadcrumbs. Using damp hands, mix well to combine and shape into walnut-sized balls, then transfer them to a tray. Cover and set aside.

★ To make the sauce, put the onions, parsley and garlic in a food processor and process until finely chopped. Transfer to a shallow frying pan/skillet large enough to hold the meatballs in a single layer. Add the tomatoes, stock, cumin, pepper, cinnamon, cayenne pepper and sugar. Stir and bring to the boil, then lower the heat and simmer, covered, for 15 minutes.

★ Nestle the meatballs in the sauce in a single layer. Cover and simmer for 20–30 minutes, until cooked through.

★ To serve, divide the meatballs and sauce between shallow soup plates or large bowls, arranging the meatballs in a ring around the perimeter. Poach or lightly fry the eggs if using (keep the yolks runny) and place one cooked egg in the middle of each bowl. Serve immediately.

meatballs

500 g/1 lb. 2 oz. minced/ground beef

100 g/1¾ cups fresh breadcrumbs

1 onion, finely diced

2 anchovy fillets, diced

grated zest of 1 small lemon

1 egg

1 teaspoon mustard

salt and freshly ground black pepper

2 tablespoons plain/all-purpose flour

broth

750 ml/3 cups chicken or vegetable stock

7 tablespoons cider vinegar

200 ml/¾ cup dry white wine

1 bay leaf

10 black peppercorns

800 g/1¾ lbs. potatoes, peeled and cut into cubes

cream sauce

50 g/3 tablespoons butter

50 g/3 tablespoons plain/all-purpose flour

100 ml/½ cup double/heavy cream

50 g/5 tablespoons capers

juice of 1 small lemon

1 teaspoon caster/granulated sugar

freshly chopped flat-leaf parsley, to garnish

serves 4

KÖNIGSBERGER KLOPSE

THESE MEATBALLS ARE A TRADITIONAL DISH FROM EASTERN GERMANY. NAMED AFTER THE FORMER PRUSSIAN CITY OF KÖNIGSBERG, THEY ARE TRADITIONALLY SERVED WITH A DELICIOUS CREAMY CAPER SAUCE AND POTATOES COOKED IN A FLAVOURFUL PEPPERY BROTH.

★ Put the beef, breadcrumbs, onion, anchovies, lemon zest, egg, mustard and seasoning in a large bowl. Using damp hands, mix together well to combine and shape the mixture into 12 golf-ball-sized balls. Lightly dust each ball with the flour.

★ Put all the broth ingredients (except the potatoes) into a large deep saucepan and bring to a simmer over a gentle heat. Carefully put the meatballs into the hot broth and simmer gently for 15–20 minutes until fully cooked. The broth should not boil as this will cause the balls to fall apart. Remove the balls from the broth and keep warm.

★ Cook the potatoes in the broth for 20–25 minutes until tender. Drain and reserve 500 ml/2 cups of the broth. Remove the bay leaf and peppercorns. (Alternatively the potatoes can be cooked separately in boiling salted water or steamed whilst the meatballs are cooking – but cooking in the broth gives them a delicious flavour.)

★ To make the sauce, melt the butter in a saucepan. Add the flour and cook for a few minutes, stirring continuously. Gradually pour in the reserved broth, bring to the boil and cook, stirring continuously until thickened. Remove from the heat. Whip the cream until slightly thickened (taking care not to over whip – it must not be stiff) then stir into the sauce with the capers, lemon juice and sugar.

★ Serve the meatballs with the cream sauce and potatoes. Sprinkle over the chopped parsley.

BITTERBALLEN

BITTERBALLEN ARE A DELICIOUS DUTCH MEATBALL, TYPICALLY SERVED WITH A DISH OF MUSTARD FOR DIPPING. THEY HAVE A SLIGHTLY GOOEY INTERIOR, WHICH MAKES A LOVELY CONTRAST TO THE CRISPY BREADCRUMB COATING. THE MIXTURE IS SOFT SO ALLOW 2 HOURS OR OVERNIGHT CHILLING TIME IN THE FRIDGE – THIS MAKES IT EASIER TO HANDLE WHEN SHAPING INTO BALLS.

2 tablespoons vegetable oil

1 onion, finely chopped

1 carrot, grated

500 g/1 lb. 2 oz. minced/ground beef

1 teaspoon grated nutmeg

juice and zest of 1 lemon

25 g/1 cup fresh flat-leaf parsley, finely chopped

salt and freshly ground black pepper

50 g/3 tablespoons butter

75 g/5 tablespoons plain/all-purpose flour

225 ml/1 scant cup whole milk

coating

150 g/1 cup plus 1 tablespoon plain/all-purpose flour

2 eggs, beaten

150 g/2¾ cups fresh breadcrumbs

mustard, for dipping

a deep-fat fryer

makes 30

★ Heat the oil in a large frying pan/skillet and fry the onion and carrot until softened. Lift out and drain and leave to cool in a bowl. Add the beef to the pan, adding a little extra oil if necessary, and fry for 4–5 minutes. Lift out and add to the onion and carrot. Stir in the nutmeg, lemon juice and zest, parsley and seasoning.

★ Melt the butter in a saucepan, stir in the flour and cook for 2–3 minutes. Gradually stir in the milk, stirring well until smooth, then bring to the boil, stirring continuously until very thick.

★ Add the sauce to the meat mixture and stir until well combined. Allow to cool, then cover the bowl with clingfilm/plastic wrap and chill in the fridge for 2 hours or preferably overnight. Using damp hands, divide the mixture into 30 golf-ball-sized balls and arrange on a large plate.

★ To coat the meatballs, dip each ball in the flour, shaking off the excess. Dip each ball into the egg, then coat each in breadcrumbs and set aside.

★ Heat the deep-fat fryer to 180°C (350°F). Fry the balls, a few at a time, for 3–4 minutes or until golden brown. Lift out and drain.

★ Serve the Bitterballen with a small dish of mustard for dipping and a glass of cold beer.

EASY SAUSAGE MEATBALLS WITH GARLIC BREAD

2 tablespoons olive oil

1 onion, chopped

2 garlic cloves, crushed

2 x 400-g/14-oz. cans chopped tomatoes

1 tablespoon tomato purée/paste

½ teaspoon caster/granulated sugar

½ teaspoon dried chilli/hot red pepper flakes

400 g/14 oz. skinless beef sausages or plain beef sausages

400 g/14 oz. dried penne, or other pasta shape

sea salt and freshly ground black pepper

freshly grated Parmesan cheese, to serve

garlic bread

1 baguette

4 tablespoons unsalted butter, softened

3 garlic cloves, crushed

1 tablespoon freshly chopped flat-leaf parsley

serves 4

THIS QUICK AND EASY MEATBALL RECIPE TAKES A MAXIMUM OF 15 MINUTES TO PREPARE AND THE RESULTS ARE DELICIOUS. GET YOUR HANDS ON SOME GOOD-QUALITY BEEF SAUSAGES AND JUST SQUEEZE OUT THE FILLING INTO WALNUT-SIZED BALLS. MAKE A VERY SIMPLE TOMATO SAUCE AND, WHILE IT IS SIZZLING AWAY, THROW THE MEATBALLS INTO THE HOT SAUCE TO COOK.

★ Heat the oil in a frying pan/skillet set over a high heat. Add the onion and garlic and cook, stirring, for 2–3 minutes, until softened. Add the tomatoes, tomato purée/paste, sugar, chilli/hot red pepper flakes and 125 ml/½ cup water and bring to the boil, then reduce to a simmer.

★ Using damp hands, squeeze the filling out of the sausage casings, if necessary, and shape into walnut-sized balls. Add these to the simmering tomato sauce. Simmer the meatballs in the sauce for 5 minutes, shaking the pan often to move the meatballs around so that they cook evenly.

★ Bring a large saucepan of lightly salted water to the boil and cook the penne for 8–10 minutes, until tender.

★ Meanwhile, to make the garlic bread, preheat the oven to 170°C (325°F) Gas 3. Cut the baguette into 4 equal portions, then cut it in half through the centre. Combine the butter, garlic and parsley in a small bowl and add a little salt. Spread the mixture on the cut side of the baguette, wrap in foil and bake in the preheated oven for about 10 minutes.

★ Drain the pasta well and return it to the warm pan/skillet. Season the meatball sauce to taste with salt and pepper. Spoon the pasta onto serving plates and top with meatballs. Sprinkle with grated Parmesan cheese and serve with the warm garlic bread on the side.

meatballs

50 g/1 scant cup fresh breadcrumbs

3 tablespoons whole milk

1 small onion

a handful of fresh flat-leaf parsley leaves

2 garlic cloves

800 g/1¾ lbs. minced/ground beef

1½ teaspoons fine sea salt

1 teaspoon dried oregano

1 teaspoon ground cumin

½ teaspoon sweet smoked paprika

1 egg, beaten

3 tablespoons extra virgin olive oil

red pepper sauce

2 red (bell) peppers

2 tablespoons extra virgin olive oil, plus extra for rubbing

1 onion, grated/minced

6 garlic cloves, crushed

¼ teaspoon cayenne pepper

5 tablespoons red wine

½ orange, well scrubbed

1 litre/4 cups tomato passata/strained tomatoes

several sprigs of thyme and 1 bay leaf, tied together with kitchen string

sea salt and freshly ground black pepper

makes about 25

MEATBALLS IN RED PEPPER SAUCE

THE COMBINATION OF ZESTY ORANGE, TOMATO AND A KICK OF HOT CHILLI GIVES THIS DISH A LOVELY, LIGHT SPANISH FEEL.

★ Preheat the oven to 220°C (425°F) Gas 7.

★ Rub the peppers with olive oil, then put on a large baking sheet lined with foil. Roast in the preheated oven for 30–40 minutes until tender and charred. Enclose them in the foil and set aside to cool. When cool, de-skin and deseed, chop coarsely and set aside. Turn the oven down to 200°C (400°F) Gas 6. Heat 2 tablespoons of the oil in a frying pan/skillet. Add the onion and a pinch of salt and cook until soft, 2–3 minutes. Add the garlic and cayenne pepper and cook, stirring, for 1 minute. Stir in the wine and squeeze in the orange juice (reserve the rest of the orange) and cook for 30 seconds. Add the tomatoes, salt, the herbs and the orange. Simmer until thick, 20–30 minutes. Add seasoning to taste. Stir in the red (bell) peppers, remove the herbs and orange and transfer to a large baking dish.

★ To make the meatballs, put the ingredients (except the oil) in a large bowl. Using damp hands, mix and shape into golf-ball-sized balls. Set on a tray.

★ Heat the 3 tablespoons oil in a large, heavy frying pan/skillet. In batches, cook the meatballs until browned evenly, about 5 minutes per batch. Using a slotted spoon, transfer the browned meatballs to the baking dish. When all the meatballs are browned, spoon some sauce over each one, then cover the baking dish with foil and bake for 20 minutes. Serve hot.

extra virgin olive oil

sea salt and freshly ground black pepper

1 tablespoon freshly chopped flat-leaf parsley

bread or quinoa, to serve

meatballs

2 teaspoons cumin seeds

2 teaspoons coriander seeds

1 clove

250 g/9 oz. minced/ground beef

200 g/7 oz. minced/ground veal

2 teaspoons grated nutmeg

2 teaspoons ground cinnamon

4 garlic cloves, crushed

6 Medjool dates, stoned/pitted and finely chopped

1 red chilli/chile, deseeded and finely chopped

2 eggs, lightly beaten

tomato sauce

1 teaspoon cumin seeds

2 red onions, halved and sliced

4 garlic cloves, crushed

1 teaspoon ground cinnamon

1 teaspoon sweet smoked paprika

100 ml/scant ½ cup red wine

2 x 400-g/14-oz. cans chopped tomatoes

2 dried bay leaves

6 sprigs fresh marjoram or oregano

3 tablespoons pure maple syrup

serves 6

SPICY SPANISH MEATBALLS

MOIST AND PACKED FULL OF AROMATIC MOORISH SPICES, THESE SPANISH MEATBALLS ARE DEEPLY SATISFYING. IT'S A PERFECT DISH FOR SHARING AMONG FRIENDS AND FAMILY WITH CRUSTY BREAD.

★ To make the meatballs, put the cumin and coriander seeds and clove in a dry pan/skillet and toast for 1–2 minutes until you can smell the aromas wafting up. Pound to a powder using a pestle and mortar.

★ Put the beef, veal, toasted spices, nutmeg, cinnamon, garlic, dates, chilli/chile and eggs in a food processor, season with a good pinch of salt and pepper and process until smooth. Transfer to a bowl, cover and allow to rest in the fridge for 30 minutes. Using damp hands, shape the mixture into golf-ball-sized meatballs, separate them and refrigerate again.

★ Meanwhile, to make the tomato sauce, toast and grind the cumin seeds as above. In the same pan, heat 2 tablespoons oil over medium heat. Add the onions and cook until translucent. If they are beginning to colour, turn down the heat a little and stir. Add the garlic, a good pinch of salt and pepper, toasted cumin, cinnamon and paprika and cook for a few minutes to release all the flavours, but do not allow the garlic to burn. Add the wine, turn the heat up to high and boil for 1–2 minutes until the wine has almost entirely evaporated. Add the chopped tomatoes and bay leaves, turn the heat down and simmer for 20 minutes, stirring occasionally.

★ Finally, add the marjoram or oregano and maple syrup. Season to taste. Some canned tomatoes can be quite bitter, in which case you can add 1–2 tablespoonfuls of maple syrup to achieve a well-rounded taste.

★ Remove the meatballs from the fridge and add to the sauce. Simmer gently for about 20 minutes or until they are cooked through. If the sauce reduces down too much, you can add a little water. Sprinkle the parsley over, then serve with bread to mop up all the juices, or on a bed of quinoa.

MEATBALL, LENTIL & CURLY KALE SOUP

THIS WONDERFUL HEARTY SOUP IS A MULTICULTURAL MIX, FEATURING DOWN-TO-EARTH BRITISH VEGETABLES, CHILLI/CHILE FROM THE EQUATOR AND TOMATOES FROM THE MEDITERRANEAN. USING GOOD QUALITY PRE-BOUGHT BEEF SAUSAGES, IT'S A QUICK OPTION TOO, ALTHOUGH YOU'RE WELCOME TO MAKE YOUR OWN MEATBALLS INSTEAD. CHARD, KALE OR ANY CABBAGE CAN BE USED FOR THIS DELICIOUS WHOLESOME DISH. IDEAL FOR A COSY WINTER SUPPER BESIDE A LOG FIRE.

400 g/14 oz. good-quality beef sausages

3 tablespoons olive oil

4 small strong onions, diced

½ swede/rutabaga or turnip, peeled and diced

1 leek, white only, sliced

2 carrots, peeled and diced

2 parsnips, peeled and diced

2 red chillies/chiles, finely chopped

2 garlic cloves, finely chopped

400 ml/1⅔ cups passata/strained tomatoes

1.3 litres/5½ cups vegetable stock

4 tablespoons tomato purée/paste

a good bunch of fresh thyme, leaves only, or tied into a bunch

150 g/¾ cup green lentils, rinsed

a large bunch of curly kale, finely sliced

sea salt and freshly ground black pepper

serves 6–8

★ To make the meatballs, carefully squeeze the meat out of your chosen sausages. Using damp hands, shape the mixture into golf-ball-sized balls.

★ Heat the oil in large saucepan, add the onions and cook for 3–4 minutes, until softened. Add the swede/rutabaga, leek, carrots and parsnips and toss around over a medium heat for about 3–5 minutes. Add the chillies/chiles and garlic to the pan, then pour over the passata/strained tomatoes and stock and add the tomato purée/paste, thyme and lentils. Simmer the soup for 15 minutes.

★ Add the meatballs carefully to the pan so that they do not get misshapen or stick together. Simmer for a further 10–15 minutes, until the meatballs are cooked through and firm. Add the kale and cook until it has reduced in volume and is tender. If you have added the thyme in a tied bunch, remove it now. Season the soup with salt and pepper, ladle into large rustic bowls and serve.

1 tablespoon extra virgin olive oil

350 g/2 cups dried couscous

700 ml/2¾ cups hot chicken or vegetable stock

plain/all-purpose flour, to coat

meatballs

125 g/4½ oz. minced/ground beef

½ small onion, finely chopped

30 g/½ cup mushrooms, finely chopped

1 garlic clove, crushed

15 g/¼ cup fresh breadcrumbs

1 teaspoon freshly chopped flat-leaf parsley or thyme

2 teaspoons vegetable oil

1 egg yolk, beaten

salt and freshly ground black pepper

five-veg sauce

2 tablespoons extra virgin olive oil

1 small onion, chopped

1 garlic clove, crushed

2 carrots, peeled and chopped

1 small courgette/zucchini, chopped

75 g/1¼ cups mushrooms, sliced

400-g/14-oz. can chopped tomatoes

125 ml/½ cup vegetable stock

1 teaspoon dried oregano

½ teaspoon brown sugar

serves 4–6

MINI MEATBALLS WITH FIVE-VEG SAUCE

THIS INGENIOUS LITTLE RECIPE IS PACKED WITH LOADS OF VEGETABLES AND ALWAYS GOES DOWN WELL WITH KIDS. THE SAUCE IS REALLY VERSATILE AND IS LOVELY AND SMOOTH STIRRED INTO PASTA.

★ Preheat the oven to 180°C (350°F) Gas 4.

★ Put the beef, onion, mushrooms, garlic, breadcrumbs, parsley, vegetable oil, egg yolk and seasoning in a bowl and mix. Using damp hands, shape the mixture into 12 mini meatballs. Put on a plate, cover and refrigerate.

★ Meanwhile, make the 5-veg sauce. Heat the oil in a saucepan, add the onion and garlic, and sauté for about 3 minutes. Add the carrots, courgette/zucchini and mushrooms and cook for about 15 minutes, or until softened.

★ Add the tomatoes, vegetable stock, oregano and brown sugar, season to taste and simmer for 10 minutes. Purée with a hand-held blender, then keep over a low heat to keep warm.

★ Put the couscous in a large bowl and pour in the hot stock. Cover and leave for 5 minutes, or until the couscous has absorbed all the liquid. Fluff up the grains with a fork.

★ Remove the mini meatballs from the fridge and lightly dust with the flour. Heat the olive oil in a large, non-stick frying pan/skillet and cook the mini meatballs for 8–10 minutes, turning frequently, until cooked through. Serve the couscous, mini meatballs and sauce together and watch it disappear!

MACARONI MEATBALL BAKE

EVERYONE LOVES A GOOD MAC 'N' CHEESE. DOTTED WITH TINY BITE-SIZED MEATBALLS, THIS IS A FAMILY FRIENDLY DISH WITH GENTLE FLAVOURS. IT IS VERY EASY TO PREPARE IN ADVANCE.

500 g/1 lb. 2 oz. dried macaroni

1 quantity béchamel sauce (see page 132)

150 g/5 oz. fresh mozzarella cheese, drained and torn into bite-sized pieces

sea salt and freshly ground black pepper

tomato sauce

2 tablespoons olive oil

1 small onion, finely chopped

1 teaspoon dried rosemary

1 garlic clove, finely chopped

400-g/14-oz. can chopped tomatoes

a pinch of sugar

meatballs

500 g/1 lb. 2 oz. minced/ground beef

20 g/⅓ cup fresh breadcrumbs

1 teaspoon dried thyme

2 teaspoons Worcestershire sauce

1 tablespoon tomato ketchup

3 tablespoons whole milk

serves 6–8

★ Cook the macaroni in a saucepan of lightly salted boiling water for 8–10 minutes until al dente and put in a large mixing bowl.

★ To make the tomato sauce, heat the oil in a large sauté pan with a lid. Add the onion and cook over a medium heat for about 5 minutes until just golden. Stir in the rosemary, garlic and 1 teaspoon of sea salt. Cook gently for 1 minute, taking care not to let the garlic burn. Add the tomatoes and sugar and simmer very gently, stirring occasionally, while you prepare the meatballs.

★ To make the meatballs, put all the ingredients in a large bowl, season with salt and pepper and mix thoroughly with your hands. If the mixture is very dry, add another tablespoon of milk; it should be soft so that the meatballs have a smooth and not crumbly texture. Using damp hands, shape the mixture into small balls, about the size of grapes.

★ Taste the sauce for seasoning and adjust as necessary. Arrange the meatballs in a single layer in the sauce, cover and simmer gently for about 20 minutes until cooked through.

★ Preheat the oven to 180°C (350°F) Gas 4.

★ Pour the hot béchamel sauce over the macaroni and mix well. Transfer to a baking dish and sprinkle over the mozzarella cheese. Spoon over the meatballs and tomato sauce in an even layer and mix the meatballs into the macaroni gently with a large wooden spoon. Bake for 20–30 minutes in the preheated oven until golden and bubbling. Serve immediately.

DEEP-DISH MEATBALL PIZZA PIE

----

pizza dough

¼ tablespoon fast-action/active dry yeast

¼ tablespoon caster/granulated sugar

60 g/¼ cup clarified butter or shortening

260 g/2 cups plain/all-purpose flour

sea salt

sauce and meatballs

1 quantity meatballs (see page 9)

1 onion, finely chopped

2 tablespoons olive oil

2 garlic cloves, thinly sliced

400-g/14-oz. can chopped tomatoes

1 pear, peeled, cored and chopped into small pieces

1 heaped teaspoon dried oregano

1 bay leaf

300 g/10½ oz. fresh mozzarella cheese, patted dry

3 tablespoons grated Parmesan cheese

non-stick 20-cm/8-inch loose-bottomed cake pan

serves 4

THIS INDULGENT CHICAGO-STYLE PIZZA IS SHAPED MORE LIKE A QUICHE AND FEATURES A CRUST THAT RESEMBLES FLAKY PASTRY AND TOPPINGS THAT COME UPSIDE DOWN. IT CAN GET A LITTLE MESSY, SO THIS VERSION IS BEST EATEN WITH A KNIFE AND FORK, A COLD BEER AND A PLAN TO GO AND DO SOME EXERCISE SOMEWHERE THE NEXT DAY.

★ To make the dough, mix 175 ml/¾ cup water with the yeast and sugar and leave for 5 minutes. Put the yeast mixture, butter or shortening, half the flour and a pinch of salt in an electric mixer with a dough hook and mix for 5 minutes. Add 100 g/¾ cup more flour and mix until a dough forms. Add the remaining flour if needed. The dough should be wet, but shouldn't stick to your hands. Put the dough in a covered bowl in the fridge to rise overnight. Remove 2–3 hours before use.

★ To make the sauce, lightly sauté the onion in a heavy-based casserole dish with the olive oil and garlic. When the onion is translucent and soft, add the tomatoes, pear pieces, oregano and bay leaf. Cook slowly for 1 hour, stirring occasionally, until the pear has dissolved into the tomato. Remove the bay leaf. Blitz with a hand-held blender until smooth.

★ Preheat the oven to its highest setting. Brown the meatballs in a frying pan/skillet and add them to the sauce. Pat out the dough in the cake pan, and up the sides. Make sure you pat the dough firmly all around the edge using your knuckles. Put three-quarters of the mozzarella cheese in the bottom of the pan. Cover with the meatballs and the sauce. Top with the remaining mozzarella and the Parmesan cheese. Bake in the preheated oven for 25–30 minutes until the crust is puffed and golden. If the inside is still at all soupy, return to the oven for another 5–10 minutes.

★ To serve, remove the sides of the cake pan and cut into quarters with a large knife or cake server.

MEATBALL & FONTINA SANDWICH

1 large ciabatta, cut into 3 thick slices, then cut widthways

4–6 slices or about 250 g/3 cups grated/shredded Fontina cheese

meatballs

225 g/8 oz. minced/ground meat, half beef and pork (or half Italian sausage instead)

30 g/½ cup fresh breadcrumbs

1 teaspoon dried oregano

1 teaspoon dried rosemary

a pinch of dried chilli/hot red pepper flakes, or more to taste

1 egg, beaten

2 tablespoons whole milk, or more if necessary

1 teaspoon salt

freshly ground black pepper

garlic tomato sauce

3 garlic cloves, crushed but not peeled

extra virgin olive oil

200 g/7 oz. passata/strained tomatoes

1 tablespoon unsalted butter

a pinch of caster/granulated sugar

salt and freshly ground black pepper

serves 3

A CONTENDER FOR THE BEST-EVER SANDWICH – MELTED CHEESE OOZES AROUND THESE SPHERES OF SEASONED BEEF TO PERFECTION.

★ Preheat the oven to 190°C (375°F) Gas 5. Line a baking sheet with parchment paper. In a mixing bowl, combine all the meatball ingredients and mix well. The mixture should be firm enough to form into balls and moist enough so they are not dry; add more milk as required. Using damp hands, shape the mixture into golf-ball-sized balls and arrange on the baking sheet. Bake until browned and cooked through, 20–30 minutes. Remove from the oven and let cool slightly. Slice in half and set aside until needed.

★ Meanwhile, prepare the sauce. Coat the garlic cloves lightly with oil, put in a small ovenproof dish and roast, at the same time as the meatballs, for 10–15 minutes, until golden and tender. Be careful not to let the garlic burn. Remove the garlic from the oven, slip the cloves from their skins and chop finely. In a small saucepan, melt the butter. Add the passata/strained tomatoes, garlic, sugar and salt and pepper. Simmer for 15 minutes. Taste and adjust the seasoning. Keep warm until needed.

★ Coat the outsides of the bread slices with oil. Assemble the sandwiches just before cooking in a large, heavy-based non-stick frying pan/skillet. You may need to cook them in batches. If space allows, put the three slices of bread, oil-side down, in the pan/skillet. Arrange half the cheese slices on top of each slice, then top with the meatball halves, dividing the pieces evenly between the sandwiches. Coat the inside of the remaining bread pieces generously with the tomato sauce and place on top of the sandwich to enclose, oil-side up.

★ Turn the heat to medium and cook the first side for 3–4 minutes until deep golden, pressing gently with a spatula. Very carefully turn and cook on the other side, for 2–3 minutes more or until deep golden brown all over. Remove from the pan/skillet and let cool for a few minutes. Insert a small wooden skewer through the middle to help hold each sandwich together.

CHILLI BEEF TARTARE & BULGUR BALLS

SOMETHING A LITTLE DIFFERENT! IF YOU LIKE 'STEAK TARTARE', YOU'LL LOVE THESE LITTLE BALLS OF RAW BEEF FROM SOUTHEASTERN TURKEY. POUNDED AND TRADITIONALLY FLAVOURED WITH AROUND 30 DIFFERENT SPICES, THEY ARE SERVED INDIVIDUALLY IN THE CUP OF A LETTUCE LEAF WITH A WEDGE OF LEMON TO SQUEEZE OVER.

150 g/1 cup minus 1 tablespoon fine bulgur

225 g/8 oz. finely minced/ground lean beef

1 onion, very finely chopped

2–3 garlic cloves, crushed

1 tablespoon tomato purée/paste

2 teaspoons finely chopped dried red chilli/chile, or paprika

2 teaspoons ground cumin

1 teaspoon each ground coriander, ground cinnamon and ground allspice

½ teaspoon ground fenugreek

sea salt and freshly ground black pepper

small bunch of fresh flat-leaf parsley, very finely chopped

to serve

1 Cos/Romaine lettuce, or 2 little gem lettuces

2 lemons, cut into wedges

2 green chillies/chiles, deseeded and finely sliced, lengthways

a bunch of fresh flat-leaf parsley leaves

serves 4–6

★ Rinse and drain the bulgur, tip it into a bowl and pour in just enough boiling water to cover it. Leave it to plump up for 10–15 minutes, then drain it thoroughly and squeeze it dry with your hands.

★ Put the minced/ground beef and bulgur into a bowl and knead it together. Add the onion, garlic, tomato purée/paste and spices, and knead well for about 5 minutes. Season with salt and pepper, add the parsley, and continue to knead for another 4–5 minutes, lifting the mixture into the air and slapping it down into the base of the bowl.

★ Arrange the lettuce leaves on a serving plate. Divide the mixture into small balls, press each one flat in the palm of your hand, pinch it between your thumb and forefinger to form a couple of indentations for the lemon juice, and arrange them on the lettuce leaves.

★ Serve the tartare patties with the lemon wedges, sliced chillies/chiles, and the parsley leaves to chew on to cut the spice. Pick up a lettuce-leaf parcel in your hand, squeeze the lemon juice into the indentation, and pop the whole thing into your mouth.

1 large onion

700 g/1½ lbs. minced/ground beef

2 garlic cloves, crushed

1 egg, lightly beaten

1 teaspoon ground cumin

½ teaspoon ground allspice

a pinch of ground cinnamon

3 tablespoons finely chopped fresh coriander/cilantro

3 tablespoons olive or groundnut oil

sea salt and freshly ground black pepper

sauce

6 tablespoons olive or groundnut oil

1 large onion, finely chopped

1 teaspoon plain/all-purpose flour

½ teaspoon ground allspice

½ teaspoon ground coriander

2 tablespoons pomegranate syrup or juice of ½ lemon

200 ml/¾ cup hot water

sea salt and freshly ground black pepper

to serve

3 tablespoons pine nuts, toasted in a dry frying pan/skillet

pitta/pita bread

makes about 20

LEBANESE MEATBALLS WITH PINE NUTS

DELICATE MEATBALLS WITH EXOTIC SPICY AROMAS ARE THE CROWN JEWELS OF LEBANESE CUISINE. THE POMEGRANATE SYRUP ADDS A NEW DIMENSION TO THIS DISH BUT CAN BE REPLACED WITH LEMON JUICE. SERVE AS PART OF A MEZZE OR AS A MAIN DISH WITH PITTA/PITA.

★ Put the onion in a food processor and pulse until coarsely chopped. Add the beef, garlic, egg, cumin, allspice, cinnamon, salt and pepper and process until smooth. Add the coriander/cilantro and pulse briefly. Transfer to a bowl. Take small spoonfuls of the mixture and shape them into walnut-sized balls using damp hands. Set aside.

★ Heat the oil in a non-stick frying pan/skillet, add the meatballs in batches and fry gently, rolling them until they brown all over.

★ Meanwhile, to make the sauce, heat the oil in a large saucepan, add the onion and sauté gently until translucent. Sprinkle with the flour, salt, pepper, allspice and ground coriander and stir for 2–3 minutes more. Add the pomegranate syrup and the water, cover and simmer for 10 minutes.

★ Add the meatballs and roll to coat them in the sauce. Cover and simmer for 10 more minutes, shaking the pan occasionally to prevent them from sticking. Sprinkle with pine nuts and serve hot with pitta/pita bread.

RAGÙ ARANCINE

75 g/5 tablespoons unsalted butter

1 onion, finely chopped

150 ml/⅔ cup dry white wine

275 g/1½ cups risotto rice, preferably arborio

900 ml/3⅔ cups hot vegetable or chicken stock

8 saffron threads or ¼ teaspoon powdered saffron

25 g/⅓ cup freshly grated Parmesan cheese

1 small egg

about 250 g/9 oz. leftover beef ragù

sea salt and freshly ground black pepper

oil, for deep-frying

coating

100 g/¾ cup plain/all-purpose flour

2 large eggs, beaten

125 g/1½ cups dried breadcrumbs

a deep-fat fryer or wok

serves 4–6

THESE CRISP GOLDEN BALLS, STUFFED WITH MEAT RAGÙ, ARE A FAMOUS SICILIAN STREET FOOD. WHEN MADE COCKTAIL-SNACK SIZE, THEY MAKE THE PERFECT BITE TO SERVE ALONGSIDE DRINKS. UNLIKE A RISOTTO, YOU SHOULD OVERCOOK THE RICE TO MAKE IT STICK TOGETHER PROPERLY.

★ Melt the butter in a large, heavy saucepan and add the onion. Cook gently for 10 minutes until soft and golden but not browned. Pour in the wine and boil hard until it has reduced and almost disappeared. Stir in the rice and coat with the butter and wine mixture. Add a ladle of stock and the saffron and simmer, stirring, until absorbed. Continue adding the stock, ladle by ladle, until all the stock has been absorbed. The rice should be very tender, thick and golden. (This should take about 20 minutes.)

★ Taste and season well with salt and pepper and stir in the Parmesan cheese. Lightly whisk the egg and beat into the risotto. Spread out on a plate and let cool completely, about 1 hour. Take 1 tablespoon cold risotto and, with damp hands, spread out in the palm of one hand. Mound a small teaspoon of beef ragù in the centre. Take another tablespoon of risotto and set over the ragù to enclose it completely. Carefully roll and smooth in your hands to form a perfect round ball (or form into a cone shape with a rounded end). Continue until all the risotto and filling has been used.

★ To make the coating, put the flour on a plate, the beaten egg in a shallow dish and the breadcrumbs in a shallow bowl. Roll the balls first in the flour, then in the egg and finally roll in the breadcrumbs until evenly coated. At this stage, they can be covered and left in the fridge for up to 1 day.

★ Heat the oil in a deep-fryer or wok until a crumb will sizzle immediately – 180°C (350°F). Fry a few arancine at a time for 3–5 minutes until deep golden. Drain on paper towels, sprinkle with salt and serve immediately (or keep warm in a low oven for up to 15 minutes).

THAI PORK & RICE SOUP

AROMATIC BROTH-BASED SOUPS SUCH AS THIS HAVE A CERTAIN PURITY TO THEM; IT MAKES THEM SIMPLE AND COMPLEX AT THE SAME TIME. AS AN ALTERNATIVE, YOU CAN MAKE THESE GARLICKY MEATBALLS INTO WONTONS IF YOU HAPPEN TO HAVE SOME WONTON WRAPPERS IN YOUR CUPBOARD. SIMPLY ENVELOPE THE MEATBALLS IN A TRIANGLE AND THEN PINCH THE ENDS OF THE WONTON WRAPPER TOGETHER. YOU COULD ALSO SWAP THE RICE IN THE SOUP FOR A HANDFUL OF DELICATE RICE NOODLES, IF YOU PREFER.

meatballs

3 garlic cloves, chopped

10 g/¼ cup fresh coriander/cilantro, leaves and stalks

450 g/1 lb. minced/ground pork

2 teaspoons fish sauce

¼ teaspoon white pepper

soup

1.2 litres/5 cups chicken stock

2-cm/¾-inch piece fresh ginger, peeled and grated

1 teaspoon caster/granulated sugar

1 tablespoon fish sauce

100 g/3½ oz. Chinese cabbage, grated

100 g/¾ cup cooked short-grain rice or 150 g/5½ oz. rice stick noodles

to serve

6 spring onions/scallions, cut into long strips

½ teaspoon sesame oil

serves 4

★ To make the meatballs, put the garlic and coriander/cilantro in a food processor and blend together until chopped. Add the pork, fish sauce and pepper and process. Using damp hands, shape the mixture into 2-cm/¾-inch meatballs. Chill until needed.

★ To make the soup, heat the stock with the ginger, sugar and fish sauce and leave it to bubble for 5 minutes. Lower in the pork meatballs and gently simmer for 3 minutes (the water should be barely bubbling). Add the Chinese cabbage and rice and simmer for a further 2 minutes, or until the meatballs are cooked through.

★ Divide the soup between 4 bowls, scatter with spring onions/scallions and drizzle with sesame oil.

meatballs

500 g/1 lb. 2 oz. minced/ground pork

2 spring onions/scallions, finely chopped

4 water chestnuts, chopped

4 garlic cloves, crushed

2.5-cm/1-inch piece fresh ginger, peeled and grated

a pinch of salt

50 ml /3 tablespoons rice wine (mirin) or dry sherry

2 tablespoons light soy sauce

1 tablespoon toasted sesame oil

1 egg, beaten

1 tablespoon cornflour/cornstarch

100 ml/⅓ cup vegetable oil, for frying

sauce

750 ml/3 cups vegetable stock

8 small (or 4 large) dried Chinese shiitake mushrooms, soaked in warm water for 15 minutes, drained

1 tablespoon light soy sauce

salt and freshly ground black pepper

250 g/9 oz. Chinese leaf or pak choi/bok choy, quartered lengthways

1 tablespoon cornflour/cornstarch, blended with 2 tablespoons cold water (optional)

2 spring onions/scallions, sliced diagonally, to serve

a little sesame oil, for drizzling

serves 4

CHINESE LIONHEAD MEATBALLS

THESE LARGE AND DELICIOUS PORK MEATBALLS COME FROM THE HUAIYANG CUISINE OF EASTERN CHINA. THE NAME DERIVES FROM THE SHAPE OF THE MEATBALLS WHICH ARE SUPPOSED TO RESEMBLE THE HEAD OF A LION – THE CABBAGE THE LION'S MANE.

★ To make the meatballs, put all the ingredients (except the vegetable oil) in a large bowl and mix together, stirring in one direction, until very thoroughly combined. The mixture should be very smooth – if not mixed sufficiently the mixture will be too soft and the meatballs will fall apart during cooking. Using damp hands, shape the mixture into 8 balls a little larger in size than a golf ball. Arrange the balls on a plate and set aside.

★ Pour the vegetable oil into a deep sauté pan, frying pan/skillet or wok and heat over a medium–high heat. Carefully lower the meatballs into the oil, a few at a time, and cook for 4–5 minutes, turning occasionally, until browned all over. Lift out and drain.

★ Put the meatballs in a large saucepan or casserole dish. Pour over the stock. Add the mushrooms, soy sauce and seasoning. Arrange the Chinese cabbage or pak choi/bok choy around the meatballs, curving them around the sides of the pan and bring to the boil. Reduce the heat to a simmer, cover the pan and cook gently for 15 minutes. (If you prefer the cabbage or pak choi/bok choy slightly firmer in texture, add it to the pan 5 minutes before the end of the cooking time.)

★ Lift out the meatballs and cabbage and arrange on a serving dish. Stir the cornflour/cornstarch mixture into the stock and bring to the boil, stirring well, to thicken. Pour the sauce over the meatballs, sprinkle on the spring onions/scallions and drizzle with a little sesame oil. Serve with sticky rice.

MINI PORK BALLS WITH CIDER SYRUP

1 litre/quart grapeseed oil

pork balls

500 g/1 lb. 2 oz. minced/ground pork

1 egg

2 teaspoons ground allspice

10 fresh sage leaves, chopped

50 g/¾ cup spring onions/scallions, chopped

1 teaspoon cayenne pepper

2 teaspoons sea salt

1 teaspoon caraway seeds

2 teaspoons tomato purée/paste

2 tablespoons goose fat or olive oil

cider syrup

500 ml/2 cups sweet apple cider

100 ml/⅓ cup balsamic vinegar

1 small red or green chilli/chile

cocktail sticks/toothpicks

makes 40–50

THESE SUBTLY SPICED PORK BALLS SERVED WITH SWEET AND STICKY CIDER SYRUP ARE ALWAYS A WINNER. THE GOOSE FAT OR OLIVE OIL KEEPS THEM SUCCULENT WHILE COOKING. IF YOU HAVE AN ELECTRIC DEEP-FAT FRYER, YOU'LL FIND THESE EVEN EASIER TO MAKE.

★ To make the pork balls, put all the ingredients in a large bowl and mix thoroughly. Using damp hands, shape the mixture into 40–50 small balls and chill in the fridge for an hour.

★ For the cider syrup, put the cider and balsamic vinegar in a heavy-based saucepan, bring to the boil, then reduce the heat and simmer until it has reduced by about half to a syrupy consistency. Add the chilli/chile and leave to infuse. (Remember to remove the chilli/chile before serving.)

★ When you are ready to cook, preheat the oven to 200°C (400°F) Gas 6.

★ Pour the grapeseed oil into a deep, heavy-based saucepan and heat for deep-frying. Alternatively, use a deep fat-fryer. To test the oil, drop in a crust of bread. If it sizzles immediately and turns golden brown it is ready; if it browns too much, turn the heat down a little. Deep-fry the pork balls in 3–4 batches for a couple of minutes. Remove with a slotted spoon and drain on paper towels. Transfer to a shallow ovenproof dish and cook in the oven for a further 5–7 minutes, until cooked all the way through. Serve with cocktail sticks/toothpick and the sticky cider syrup in a small bowl for dipping.

VIETNAMESE PORK BALL SKEWERS

1 lemongrass stalk

500 g/1 lb. 2 oz. minced/ground pork

125 g/4½ oz. pork belly, minced/ground

25 g/½ cup fresh breadcrumbs

6 kaffir lime leaves, very finely sliced

2 garlic cloves, crushed

2-cm/¾-inch piece fresh ginger, grated

1 red chilli/chile, deseeded and chopped

2 tablespoons Thai fish sauce

to serve

lettuce leaves

a handful of fresh herb leaves, such as mint, coriander/cilantro and Thai basil

sweet chilli/chile sauce (page 131)

a barbecue/grill

4 wooden skewers soaked in cold water for 30 minutes

serves 4

LIKE MANY VIETNAMESE DISHES, THESE DELICIOUS BARBECUED/GRILLED PORK SKEWERS ARE SERVED WRAPPED IN A LETTUCE LEAF WITH LOTS OF FRESH HERBS AND SWEET CHILLI/CHILE SAUCE TO DRIZZLE OVER.

★ Using a sharp knife, trim the lemongrass stalks to about 15 cm/6 inches in length, then remove and discard the tough outer leaves. Chop the inner stalk very finely.

★ Put the minced/ground pork, pork belly and breadcrumbs into a bowl, then add the lemongrass, kaffir lime leaves, garlic, ginger, chilli/chile and fish sauce and mix well. Allow to marinate in the fridge for at least 1 hour.

★ Using damp hands, shape the mixture into 20 small balls and carefully thread 5 onto each of the soaked wooden skewers. Preheat a barbecue/grill, then brush the grill rack with oil. Cook the skewers for 5–6 minutes, turning half-way through until well cooked.

★ Serve the pork balls wrapped in the lettuce leaves with the mixed herbs and sweet chilli/chile sauce.

GARLIC CHIVE MEATBALLS

STEAMING THESE MEATBALLS, RATHER THAN FRYING, IS AN EASIER AND HEALTHY WAY OF COOKING THEM. SERVE WITH RICE OR NOODLES AND CHINESE GREENS SUCH AS PAK CHOI/BOK CHOY OR GAI LAN (ALSO KNOWN AS CHINESE BROCCOLI OR CHINESE KALE). THE CHILLI/CHILE, SOY AND SESAME DIPPING SAUCE ADDS A NICE BIT OF RICHNESS.

500 g/1 lb. 2 oz. minced/ground pork

25 g/1 oz. Chinese or garlic chives, finely chopped

1 garlic clove, finely chopped

1-cm/½-inch piece fresh ginger, peeled and finely chopped

1 egg white

1 tablespoon light soy sauce

1 teaspoon salt

½ teaspoon ground white or black pepper

1 teaspoon sesame oil

2 teaspoons cornflour/cornstarch

chilli/chile dipping sauce

3 tablespoons light soy sauce

1 teaspoon sesame oil

½ red chilli/chile, deseeded and finely chopped

a steamer

serves 4

★ Blend all the meatball ingredients together in a food processor until thoroughly mixed. Using damp hands to prevent sticking, shape the mixture into small meatballs, each the size of a large marble.

★ Steam the meatballs for 20 minutes until cooked through.

★ Mix together the dipping sauce ingredients. Serve the meatballs with the chilli/chile dipping sauce.

FRIKADELLE

A TRADITIONAL DISH IN SCANDINAVIA, HOLLAND AND GERMANY, FRIKADELLE ARE FLATTENED MEAT AND POTATO DUMPLINGS. THE ANCHOVIES ACT LIKE FISH SAUCE IN SOUTH-EAST ASIAN COOKING – AS A SEASONING, RATHER THAN A FLAVOURING.

75 g/2½ oz. mashed potato

250 g/9 oz. minced/ground pork*

125 g/4½ oz. minced/ground veal*

125 g/4½ oz. minced/ground lamb*

70 g/1 scant cup dried breadcrumbs

60 ml /4 tablespoons single/light cream

1 egg, beaten

a pinch of freshly grated nutmeg

1 canned anchovy fillet, mashed

a pinch of freshly ground allspice

3 tablespoons butter

1 small onion, finely chopped

2 tablespoons vegetable oil

sea salt and freshly ground black pepper

rosemary sprigs, for serving

makes about 30

*Note: The traditional meat combination is 250 g/9 oz. each of minced/ground pork and veal.

★ Put the potato in a bowl with the meat, breadcrumbs, cream, egg, nutmeg, anchovy, allspice, a large pinch of salt and a good grinding of black pepper. Mix well.

★ Heat 1 tablespoon of the butter in a frying pan/skillet, add the onion and sauté until softened and translucent. Stir into the meat mixture.

★ Wet your hands, take 1 tablespoon of the mixture, roll it between your palms to form a ball, then flatten it slightly. Repeat until all the mixture has been used. Arrange the balls apart on a tray, cover with clingfilm/plastic wrap and chill for about 1 hour.

★ Heat the remaining butter and the oil in a heavy-based frying pan/skillet, then fry the meatballs, spaced apart, in batches, until browned on both sides. Shake them from time to time. Remove and drain on crumpled paper towels.

★ Serve with cocktail sticks/toothpicks or rosemary sprigs – the rosemary gives a wonderful fragrance to the frikadelle.

★ Alternatively, serve with a Chilli/Chile Dipping Sauce (page 43), or in hamburger buns, in pitta/pita breads, in tortilla wraps or in ciabatta pockets with your choice of salad leaves and sauce.

sweet and sour sauce

2 teaspoons peanut oil

1 garlic clove, finely chopped

1 red chilli/chile, deseeded and finely chopped

2 tablespoons roasted peanuts, finely chopped

1 tablespoon Thai fish sauce

2 tablespoons rice wine vinegar

2 tablespoons hoisin sauce

4 tablespoons coconut milk

1–2 teaspoons caster/granulated sugar, to taste

a pinch of sea salt

kofta (meatballs)

2 teaspoons peanut or sesame oil

4 shallots, finely chopped

2 garlic cloves, finely chopped

450 g/1 lb. minced/ground pork

2 tablespoons Thai fish sauce

2 teaspoons five-spice powder

2 teaspoons caster/granulated sugar

2 handfuls of fresh breadcrumbs

sea salt and freshly ground black pepper

to serve

noodles

a small bunch of fresh coriander/cilantro

a packet of short wooden or bamboo skewers, soaked in water before use

serves 4

ASIAN PORK KOFTA

TRY THESE MEATBALL KEBABS WITH THE SWEET AND SOUR SAUCE AND STIR-FRIED NOODLES & BEANSPROUTS ON PAGE 140.

★ To make the sauce, heat the oil in a small wok or heavy-based frying pan/skillet. Stir in the garlic and chilli/chile and, when they begin to colour, add the peanuts. Stir for a few minutes until the natural oil from the peanuts begins to weep. Add all the remaining ingredients (except the sugar and salt) along with 100 ml/⅓ cup water. Let the mixture bubble up for 1 minute. Adjust the sweetness and seasoning to taste with sugar and some salt and set aside.

★ To make the meatballs, heat the oil in a wok or a heavy-based frying pan/skillet. Add the shallots and garlic. When they begin to brown, turn off the heat and leave to cool. Put the minced/ground pork into a bowl, tip in the stir-fried shallot and garlic, fish sauce, five-spice powder and sugar and season with a little salt and lots of pepper. Using your hands, knead the mixture so it is well combined. Cover and chill in the fridge for 2–3 hours. Knead the mixture again then tip in the breadcrumbs. Knead well to bind.

★ Using damp hands, divide the mixture into roughly 20 portions and shape into balls. Thread them onto the prepared skewers. Prepare a charcoal or conventional grill/broiler. Cook the skewers for 3–4 minutes on each side, turning them from time to time, until browned.

★ Reheat the sauce. Serve the kofta with noodles and the hot sweet and sour sauce on the side for dipping.

WURST MEATBALLS

GERMANY DEVELOPED THE 'WURST' PROCESS FOR CURING SAUSAGES, BUT MANY WOULD ARGUE THAT IT'S THE BEST... (PAUSE FOR LAUGHTER). IN THE PAST, GERMANY EXCELLED AT SMOKING MEAT AND THEY STILL MAKE EXCELLENT SAUSAGES TODAY. WITHOUT A SMOKER AT HOME OR SAUSAGE CASINGS HANDY, IT'S NOT EASY TO RECREATE THEM, BUT HERE'S A RECIPE THAT USES THE INGREDIENTS AND FLAVOURS FOR RAW 'ROHWURST' SAUSAGE – IT CERTAINLY DOES MAKES LOVELY MEATBALLS. SERVE THESE ALONGSIDE PASTA, RICE AND VEGETABLES OR EVEN THE FANCY MASHED POTATOES ON PAGE 134.

200 g/7 oz. minced/ground pork

a pinch of ground mace

a pinch of ground ginger

a pinch of ground nutmeg

a pinch each of sea salt and freshly ground black pepper

½ egg, beaten

1 teaspoon dried milk powder

2 teaspoons dried breadcrumbs

serves 2

★ Put all the ingredients into a bowl and mix them together really well with damp hands. Divide and shape the mixture into 8 even-sized meatballs.

★ To cook the meatballs, either fry them in a frying pan/skillet over a high heat or cook them under a preheated high grill/broiler for 12–15 minutes, turning occasionally.

★ Once cooked, combine the meatballs with a sauce of your choice and serve with cooked pasta or potatoes, as you wish.

GOULASH MEATBALLS

THESE SMOKY AND AROMATIC HUNGARIAN-STYLE MEATBALLS WILL NEVER FAIL TO PLEASE A HUNGRY CROWD – JUST DON'T FORGET THE COOLING DOLLOP OF SOUR CREAM ON THE SIDE. THEY ARE GREAT TO MAKE IN ADVANCE AND CAN BE FROZEN IN INDIVIDUAL PORTIONS.

sauce

⅔ onion, very finely chopped

250 ml/1 cup chicken stock

2 garlic cloves, crushed

1 red and 1 green (bell) pepper, deseeded and diced

2 teaspoons paprika

400-g/14-oz. can chopped tomatoes

1 tablespoon tomato purée/paste

sea salt and freshly ground black pepper

meatballs

⅓ onion, very finely chopped

500 g/1 lb. 2 oz. minced/ground pork

1 slice wholemeal/wholewheat bread, processed to crumbs

1 teaspoon paprika

1 teaspoon smoked paprika

1 teaspoon dried sage

to serve

150 g/5½ oz. wholemeal/wholewheat spaghetti

250 g/9 oz. shredded green cabbage

6 teaspoons sour cream

serves 6

★ Start the sauce by cooking the onion in 4 tablespoons of the stock in a covered casserole dish for 4–5 minutes until softened. Stir in the garlic, peppers and paprika and cook for 1 minute, then add the tomatoes, tomato purée/paste and the remaining stock. Season and simmer, uncovered, for 10 minutes.

★ While the sauce is cooking, mix the meatball ingredients together, season and, using damp hands, shape into 24 small balls.

★ Brown the meatballs in two batches in a non-stick frying pan/skillet, then add to the sauce and simmer for 20 minutes.

★ Cook the spaghetti in a large saucepan of lightly salted boiling water for 7 minutes, then stir in the cabbage and cook for a further 5 minutes. Drain and divide the pasta and cabbage between warmed bowls. Spoon the meatballs and sauce over the pasta and top each serving with a teaspoon of sour cream.

faggots

500 g/1 lb. 2 oz. minced/ground pork

100 g/3½ oz. lamb or pigs liver, finely chopped

100 g/3½ oz. streaky/fatty bacon, finely chopped

1 onion, finely chopped

2 teaspoons dried thyme

1 teaspoon dried sage

100 g/1¾ cups fresh breadcrumbs

15 g/½ cup freshly chopped flat-leaf parsley

salt and freshly ground black pepper

12 rashers/slices streaky/fatty bacon

onion gravy

1 tablespoon vegetable oil

2 onions, finely chopped

500 ml/2 cups ale

200 ml/¾ cup hot beef stock

2 tablespoons balsamic vinegar

2 teaspoons Worcestershire sauce

2 teaspoons mixed dried herbs

sea salt and freshly ground black pepper

4 teaspoons cornflour/cornstarch

a large baking sheet, greased

serves 4–6

FAGGOTS

FAGGOTS ARE AN OLD-FASHIONED BRITISH DISH, THOUGHT TO HAVE ORIGINATED IN THE MIDLANDS. THEY WERE POPULAR THROUGHOUT THE YEARS OF RATIONING DURING THE SECOND WORLD WAR AS THEY MADE AN ECONOMICAL MEAL. AS A RESULT, FAGGOTS GOT A RATHER BAD PRESS AND FELL OUT OF FAVOUR. HOWEVER, THIS DELICIOUS DISH IS ENJOYING A REVIVAL THESE DAYS, AND THIS RECIPE IS A MODERN-DAY TAKE ON THE TRADITIONAL VERSION. GIVE IT A TRY!

★ Preheat the oven to 180°C (350°F) Gas 4.

★ Place all the faggot ingredients (except the bacon rashers/slices) in a large bowl and mix together until thoroughly combined. Using damp hands, shape the mixture into 12 large golf-ball-sized balls.

★ Stretch the bacon rashers/slices slightly with the back of a knife. Wrap a bacon rasher/slice around each ball. Arrange the faggots on the baking sheet.

★ Bake the faggots for 45–50 minutes until well browned.

★ Meanwhile, make the onion gravy. Heat the oil in a large saucepan. Add the onions and cook over a moderate heat for 15 minutes until softened and lightly brown. Stir in the ale, stock, vinegar, Worcestershire sauce, herbs and seasoning. Bring to the boil, reduce the heat and simmer for 5 minutes, stirring occasionally. Blend the cornflour/cornstarch with 4 teaspoons water to make a smooth paste. Add a few spoonfuls of the hot liquid, stir well to combine and add to the gravy. Bring to the boil, stirring continuously until thickened. Add more thickener if necessary.

★ Serve the faggots with the onion gravy, mashed potato and mushy peas.

PORK & FENNEL MEATBALLS

THIS AUTHENTIC ITALIAN RECIPE TELLS YOU HOW TO MAKE YOUR OWN MINCED/GROUND MEAT FROM A COMBINATION OF PORK CUTS DESIGNED TO GIVE THE BEST TEXTURE. THESE BALLS ARE BURSTING WITH FLAVOUR FROM FENNEL SEEDS AND GARLIC. SERVE AS IT IS OR DRESS THE PASTA WITH THE SAUCE AS A FIRST COURSE AND EAT THE MEATBALLS AS A COURSE ON THEIR OWN AS IS TRADITIONAL.

450 g/1 lb. pork shoulder or leg

225-g/8-oz. piece unsmoked gammon

225 g/8 oz. pork belly

2 garlic cloves, crushed

2 tablespoons fennel seeds

a large pinch of dried chilli/hot red pepper flakes

2 teaspoons sea salt

1 tablespoon caster/granulated sugar

2 tablespoons coarsely crushed black pepper

olive oil (see method)

150 ml/⅔ cup dry white wine

400-g/14-oz. can chopped tomatoes

200 ml/¾ cup passata/strained tomatoes

sea salt and freshly ground black pepper

serves 6

★ Trim the pork shoulder or leg, gammon and pork belly of any skin or connective tissue. Cut the meat into large chunks, then pass them through the coarse blade of an electric mincer or chop very finely with a large sharp knife or cleaver (do not use a food processor).

★ Put the meat in a large bowl, add the garlic, fennel seeds, chilli/hot red pepper flakes, salt, sugar and pepper. Mix well with clean hands or a large wooden spoon. At this stage, the sausage meat is ready to use, but you can cover the bowl and let it mature in the fridge overnight.

★ Using damp hands, shape the mixture into walnut-sized meatballs.

★ To cook, heat 2 tablespoons of the oil in a frying pan/skillet and quickly brown the meatballs all over, in batches if necessary. Remove to a plate with a slotted spoon and add the wine. Deglaze the pan and let the wine bubble until there is only 1 tablespoon left. Add the chopped tomatoes and passata/strained tomatoes, salt and pepper. Bring back to the boil, then return the meatballs to the sauce. Part-cover with a lid and simmer for 30–40 minutes, topping up with water if the sauce is becoming too dry. Serve as it is or dress the pasta with the sauce as a first course and eat the meatballs as a course on their own.

PORK & COURGETTE/ZUCCHINI MEATBALLS

500 g/1 lb. 2 oz. courgettes/
zucchini, topped and tailed

500 g/1 lb. 2 oz. minced/ground
pork

2 generous tablespoons dry white
breadcrumbs

1 teaspoon fennel seeds, crushed

1 red chilli/chile, deseeded and
finely chopped

1 fat garlic clove, finely chopped

zest of 1 small lemon

1–2 teaspoons chopped lemon
thyme or oregano

olive oil, for roasting and frying

1 large aubergine/eggplant, cut
into 1–2-cm/½–1-inch cubes

1½ teaspoons cumin seeds

2 tablespoons honey

15 g/½ cup freshly chopped dill

½ teaspoon ground sumac
(optional)

200 ml/1 scant cup Greek-style,
strained yogurt

2 lemons, halved

seeds from 1 pomegranate

sea salt and freshly ground black
pepper

serves 4

THE ADDITION OF COURGETTE/ZUCCHINI KEEPS THESE LITTLE
MEATBALLS LIGHT AND MOIST. THEY ARE PARTNERED BY A WARM
POMEGRANATE AND ROASTED AUBERGINE/EGGPLANT SALAD,
CARAMELIZED LEMON HALVES AND YOGURT DRESSING. THOUGH YOU
COULD SERVE THEM IN A TOMATO SAUCE WITH PASTA, IF PREFERRED.

★ Coarsely grate about 200 g/7 oz. of the courgettes/zucchini, toss with
1 teaspoon salt, then leave to drain in a colander for 45–60 minutes. Rinse,
transfer to a dry, clean kitchen cloth and squeeze dry. Put the pork, grated
courgette/zucchini, breadcrumbs, crushed fennel seeds, chilli/chile, garlic,
lemon zest and thyme in a bowl with ½ teaspoon salt and a grinding of black
pepper. Using damp hands, mix well to combine and shape into walnut-sized
balls. Chill in the fridge until ready to cook.

★ Meanwhile, preheat the oven to 200°C (400°F) Gas 6. Cut the remaining
courgettes/zucchini into cubes of a similar size to the aubergine/eggplant.
Toss the courgettes/zucchini and aubergines/eggplant with 2 tablespoons
olive oil and season well. Toast the cumin seeds in a small, dry frying
pan/skillet over a low heat until fragrant, then crush in a mortar with a
pestle. Sprinkle half over the vegetables and roast them, uncovered, in the
preheated oven for about 30–35 minutes, stirring once, until tender and nicely
browned. Drizzle over the honey, then roast for a further 5–7 minutes. Turn
into a bowl and toss with most of the dill and sumac (if using). Beat the
yogurt with the remaining cumin, then season to taste.

★ Cook the meatballs in very shallow oil in a non-stick frying pan/skillet for
about 8–10 minutes until browned on all sides and cooked through. Remove
from the pan and keep warm. Wipe out the pan, then add the halved lemons,
cut-side down, and fry briefly until browned and caramelized on the cut side.
Top the salad with the remaining dill and the pomegranate seeds. Serve the
meatballs piping hot, with the caramelized lemon halves and the salad and
yogurt on the side.

PANCETTA & FENNEL PUFFS

THESE *COCCOLI* ('LITTLE DARLINGS'!) ARE A TYPE OF TASTY SAVOURY DOUGHNUT FLAVOURED WITH PANCETTA. THEY ARE DEEP-FRIED UNTIL CRISP ON THE OUTSIDE AND BEAUTIFULLY SOFT INSIDE. BE SURE TO KEEP THEM WARM IN THE OVEN IF COOKING BATCHES TO MAKE SURE THEY ARE PIPING HOT WHEN YOU SERVE THEM. GRINDING A SPRINKLE OF FENNEL SEEDS OVER IS A REALLY SPECIAL FINISHING TOUCH, TOO.

200 ml/¾ cup whole milk

50 g/3 tablespoons pure lard, roughly chopped

40 g/2 tablespoons plus 2 teaspoons fresh yeast or 1 sachet fast-action dried yeast

400 g/3 cups Italian '00' flour

50 g/1¾ oz. pancetta, finely diced

1 teaspoon fennel seeds, lightly crushed

vegetable or olive oil, for deep-frying

sea salt

deep-fat fryer

makes 30–40 puffs

★ Put the milk and lard in a saucepan and heat gently until the lard has melted. Don't let the milk get too hot. Crumble in the fresh yeast (if using) and whisk until dissolved. Sift the flour and a good pinch of salt into a bowl and make a well in the centre. If you are using fast-action dried yeast, stir it into the flour now. Pour in the warm milk mixture, and add the pancetta and fennel seeds. Mix to a soft dough, adding more flour, if necessary. Form into a ball, cover with clingfilm/plastic wrap or a damp kitchen cloth and leave to rise for 2 hours or until doubled in size.

★ Heat the oil in the deep-fat fryer to 180°C (350°F). A piece of stale bread dropped in should sizzle and turn golden in a few seconds.

★ Uncover the dough, punch out the air and knead for 1 minute. Using damp hands, pull off small walnut-sized pieces of dough and roll into rough balls. Fry in batches for about 2–3 minutes until pale brown and puffy. Drain well and tip onto paper towels. Sprinkle with salt and serve while they are still hot.

SCOTCH QUAILS' EGGS

BITE-SIZED EGGS ARE MORE FUN THAN THE LARGER VARIETY, AND QUAILS' EGGS ARE PACKED WITH PROTEIN TOO. A NICE WAY TO SERVE THEM IS TO MIX A LITTLE MUSTARD WITH MAYO AND SERVE ON THE SIDE AS A DIP. THEY MAKE A GREAT ADDITION TO A PICNIC.

12 quails' eggs

600 g/1⅓ lbs. good-quality pork sausages

1 tablespoon finely chopped fresh flat-leaf parsley

1 tablespoon finely chopped fresh thyme (optional)

1 egg yolk, beaten, plus 1 whole egg

1 tablespoon plain/all-purpose flour

4 tablespoons whole milk

75 g/1 cup fine breadcrumbs

sunflower oil, for frying

sea salt and freshly ground black pepper

makes 12

★ Bring a small saucepan of water to the boil and gently lower in the quails' eggs. Boil for 100 seconds, then plunge the boiled eggs immediately into cold water to stop them from continuing to cook. Once cold, one at a time, roll each egg gently along a work surface with the flat of your palm until the shell is all crackled, then peel away the shell. Set the peeled eggs aside until needed.

★ Remove the skins from the sausages and discard and put the sausage meat in a large mixing bowl with the parsley, thyme, if using, and egg yolk. Season with salt and pepper and stir to combine. Using damp hands, shape the mixture into 12 equal-sized portions.

★ Get 3 shallow bowls ready, the first holding the plain/all-purpose flour seasoned with salt and pepper, the next with a whole egg beaten with the milk, and the last bowl filled with the breadcrumbs.

★ Take a portion of sausage meat and make a patty with it in your palm. Place a quail's egg in the centre and gently mould the sausage meat around it before rolling it into a ball between your palms. Repeat with the rest of the sausage meat and quails' eggs. Roll each scotch egg firstly in seasoned flour, then dip it in the egg wash before coating it in the breadcrumbs.

★ Pour the oil into a saucepan and bring up to smoking hot temperature, (around 180°C/350°F). Fry a few eggs at a time for about 4 minutes until they are golden brown all over. Transfer to a plate lined with paper towels to soak up any excess oil and leave to cool before serving.

CUBAN *PAPAS RELLENAS*

1.5 kg/3⅓ lbs. potatoes, peeled and cut into chunks

picadillo

1 tablespoon vegetable oil

1 small onion, finely chopped

2 garlic cloves, crushed

225 g/8 oz. minced/ground lamb

50 g/1¾ oz. cooking chorizo sausage, chopped

2 teaspoons ground cumin

2 teaspoons paprika

1 tablespoon tomato purée/paste

1 tablespoon vinegar

sea salt and freshly ground black pepper

coating

100 g/¾ cup plain/all-purpose flour

2 eggs, beaten

150 g/2½ cups fresh breadcrumbs

a deep-fat fryer

serves 4–6

THESE TRADITIONAL CUBAN SNACKS – POTATO BALLS STUFFED WITH A TASTY MEAT FILLING CALLED *PICADILLO* – ARE DEEP FRIED FOR CRISPNESS. THEY ARE EQUALLY DELICIOUS EATEN HOT OR COLD.

★ Boil or steam the potatoes until tender. Drain and mash until smooth, adding salt to taste. Leave to cool completely.

★ To make the *picadillo*, first heat the oil in a large saucepan. Add the onion and garlic and fry for a few minutes until softened. Add the lamb and chorizo and fry until evenly browned. Stir in the cumin, paprika, tomato purée/paste, vinegar and salt and pepper. Cover and cook over a medium heat for 10–15 minutes, stirring occasionally until the meat is fully cooked. Drain off any excess fat and liquid and allow to cool completely.

★ To make the balls, place the cold potato on a lightly floured surface and using floured hands divide into two large portions. This makes it easier to handle. Shape each portion into a thick sausage then cut each into 8 pieces so you have 16 in total. Lightly flour your hands and shape each piece of potato into a ball. Cut each ball in half. Shape each half into a bowl or cup. Place a spoonful of the *picadillo* inside one half, position the second half on top and press the two halves together, shaping carefully to completely encase the filling inside the ball. Make sure the ball is completely sealed.

★ Dust each ball in flour, shaking off the excess. Dip in the egg, then roll in the breadcrumbs to coat completely. Place the balls on a plate or tray, cover with clingfilm/plastic wrap and chill in the fridge for 30 minutes.

★ Preheat the deep-fat fryer to 180°C (350°F).

★ Cook the balls a few at a time for 3–4 minutes until golden brown. Drain on paper towels. Serve hot or cold with a bowl of hot sauce, such as Frank's Hot Sauce or Sriracha or simply with a salad.

MINI MEATBALLS STUFFED WITH ROASTED PISTACHIOS

2–3 tablespoons pistachios, shelled

250 g/9 oz. lean minced/ground lamb

1 onion, finely chopped

2 garlic cloves, crushed

2 teaspoons ground cinnamon

a small bunch of fresh flat-leaf parsley, finely chopped

sea salt and freshly ground black pepper

sunflower oil

1–2 lemons, cut into wedges

serves 4–6

MEATBALLS ARE PREPARED DAILY IN THE MIDDLE EASTERN REGION AS MEZZE, STREET FOOD AND AS MAIN COURSES. THEY ARE USUALLY MADE FROM MINCED/GROUND LAMB OR BEEF AND, ON OCCASION, MINCED/GROUND CHICKEN. THESE MINI ONES, CALLED *CIZBIZ*, ARE PERFECT MEZZE BALLS CONTAINING A BITE OF ROASTED PISTACHIO IN THE MIDDLE, WHICH GIVES A LOVELY TEXTURE AND PRETTY GREEN COLOUR. SERVE WITH WEDGES OF LEMON TO SQUEEZE OVER TO TASTE.

★ In a small heavy-based frying pan/skillet, toast the pistachios for 1–2 minutes, until they emit a nutty aroma. Using a pestle and mortar, crush most of them lightly to break them into small pieces.

★ In a bowl, pound the minced/ground lamb with the onion, garlic and cinnamon. Knead it with your hands and slap the mixture down into the base of the bowl to knock out the air. Add the parsley and seasoning and knead well to make sure it is thoroughly mixed.

★ Using damp hands, take cherry-sized portions of the mixture and roll them into balls. Indent each ball with your finger, right into the middle, and fill the hollow with a few of the crushed pistachios, and seal it by squeezing the mixture over it and then rolling the ball once more.

★ Heat a thin layer of oil in a heavy-based frying pan/skillet. Place the meatballs in the pan/skillet and cook them on all sides, until nicely browned. Drain on paper towels, sprinkle with the remaining crushed pistachios, and serve with lemon wedges to squeeze over them.

meatballs

2 tablespoons vegetable oil

1 onion, finely chopped

2 garlic cloves, crushed

500 g/1 lb. 2 oz. minced/ground lamb

30 g/1 cup freshly chopped mint leaves

1 teaspoon ground cumin

1 teaspoon ground coriander

grated zest of 1 lemon

50 g/1 scant cup fresh white breadcrumbs

salt and freshly ground black pepper

50-g/1¾-oz. piece of feta cheese, cut into 4

2 tablespoons plain/all-purpose flour, for dusting

2–3 tablespoons vegetable oil, for frying

red onion relish

1 tablespoon olive oil

200 g/7 oz. red onions, finely sliced

2 teaspoons brown sugar

1 tablespoon balsamic vinegar

to serve

hamburgers buns, lightly toasted

watercress

makes 4

GIANT LAMB & MINT BALLS

MINT, LAMB AND FETA ARE A MATCH MADE IN HEAVEN IN THESE HUGE BURGER-MEATBALL HYBRIDS. THEY ARE EASY TO MAKE AND THE STAR OF THE SHOW SERVED AT A BARBECUE OR GRILL PARTY.

★ Heat the oil in a heavy-based frying pan/skillet. Add the onion and garlic and fry gently for 5–10 minutes until softened. Cool slightly.

★ Put the minced/ground lamb into a bowl and add the onion and garlic, mint, cumin, coriander, lemon zest, breadcrumbs, salt and pepper and mix together very well with your hands to bind the mixture together.

★ Divide the mixture into 4 even-sized portions. With floured hands, flatten each piece into a thick disc.

★ Cut each piece of feta cheese into 6–8 small cubes. Place one portion of feta cubes in the centre of each disc. Mould the meat mixture into a ball over the feta so it is completely enclosed. Lightly flour your hands and mould and flatten each ball again slightly so you have 4 large burgers approx 2.5 cm/1 inch thick.

★ Heat a griddle or frying pan/skillet and add a little oil. Add the burgers to the pan/skillet, and cook for 8–10 minutes until firm, then turn over and cook the second side for 8–10 minutes or until fully cooked and browned and the juices run clear. Lift out and drain on paper towels.

★ For the red onion relish, heat the oil in a large heavy-based frying pan/skillet. Add the onions and cook over a gentle heat for 20–25 minutes until very soft. Add the sugar and vinegar and cook for a further 10 minutes.

★ Serve the burgers, topped with the relish, in toasted hamburger buns, garnished with watercress.

GREEK LAMB BALLS WITH FAVA

fava

180 g/1 cup dried yellow split peas, rinsed

1 bay leaf

1 teaspoon salt

2 tablespoons dry white wine

3 garlic cloves, crushed

60 ml/¼ cup extra virgin olive oil

2 teaspoons dried oregano

2 tablespoons red wine vinegar

2 tomatoes, finely diced

1 tablespoon capers, fried for 30 seconds in 1 tablespoon olive oil

freshly ground black pepper

lamb meatballs

600 g/1¼ lbs. minced/ground lamb

1 teaspoon ground cinnamon

3 garlic cloves, crushed

50 g/1 cup fresh breadcrumbs

2 tablespoons oregano, chopped

1 egg, lightly beaten

1 teaspoon cracked black pepper

sea salt

to serve

toasted pitta/pita bread

tomato and red onion salad

makes 32 meatballs

FAVA IS AN UNSUNG HERO OF THE MEZZE PLATTER. SCENTED WITH GARLIC AND BAY, IT PAIRS EXTREMELY WELL WITH LAMB MEATBALLS AND GRILLED/BROILED MEAT. IT'S COMFORTING AND DELICIOUS BOTH COLD AND WARM, AND, PERHAPS BEST OF ALL IN THESE LEAN TIMES, IT'S VERY, VERY CHEAP. ANOTHER THING WE CAN THANK THE GREEKS FOR (ALONG WITH DEMOCRACY, THAT IS). SERVE ALONGSIDE PITTA/ PITA AND A FRESH TOMATO AND RED ONION SALAD.

★ For the fava, put the split peas in a large saucepan and cover with cold water by 5 cm/2 inches. Bring to the boil. Reduce the heat to medium and skim off any scum that appears. Add the bay leaf and simmer for 40 minutes. Add the salt and simmer for 20 more minutes until the split peas are soft. Drain off any excess liquid and remove the bay leaf.

★ Add the white wine, garlic and olive oil and blend with a hand-held blender until smooth. Allow to cool. Season with dried oregano, red wine vinegar, salt and black pepper. Top with finely diced tomatoes, fried capers and a drizzle of olive oil and serve alongside the meatballs.

★ For the meatballs, preheat the oven to 200°C (400°F) Gas 6. Line a baking sheet with baking parchment.

★ In a large bowl, combine the lamb with the rest of the ingredients and season with salt and pepper. Using damp hands, mix well and shape the mixture into walnut-sized balls. Place on the prepared baking sheet and bake for 15–20 minutes or until cooked through.

★ Serve with the fava, toasted pitta/pita bread and a well-seasoned tomato and onion salad.

KEFTA TAGINE WITH EGGS & CUMIN

225 g/8 oz. minced/ground lamb

1 onion, finely chopped

1 teaspoon dried mint

1–2 teaspoons ras-el-hanout spice mix

½ teaspoon cayenne pepper

1 small bunch of fresh flat-leaf parsley, finely chopped and 1 small bunch, roughly chopped, to serve

sea salt and freshly ground black pepper

1 tablespoon butter

¼–½ teaspoon salt

1 teaspoon cayenne pepper or chopped dried chillies/chiles

4 medium or large eggs

1–2 teaspoons cumin seeds, dry-roasted and ground

serves 4

VARIATIONS OF THIS GREAT STREET DISH CAN BE FOUND THROUGHOUT MOROCCO. IN MANY HOUSEHOLDS, KEFTA (POACHED MEATBALLS) ARE PREPARED IN BATCHES AS A HANDY SNACK. THEY ARE USUALLY QUITE FIERY, SO SERVE WITH BREAD, PARSLEY AND COOLING FRESH YOGURT TO TEMPER THEIR HEAT.

★ To make the kefta, put the minced/ground lamb, onion, mint, ras-el-hanout, cayenne pepper and finely chopped parsley in a bowl, season to taste with salt and pepper and mix well together. Using damp hands, knead the mixture and mould it into small balls, roughly the size of a quail's egg, so that you end up with about 12 balls.

★ Fill a tagine or casserole dish with water and bring it to the boil. Carefully drop in the kefta, a few at a time, and poach them for about 10 minutes, turning them so that they are cooked on all sides. Remove them with a slotted spoon and drain on paper towels. Reserve roughly 300 ml/2¼ cups of the cooking liquid. (If not using the kefta immediately, transfer them to a plate to cool and store in the fridge for 2–3 days.)

★ Add the butter to the reserved cooking liquid in the tagine or casserole dish and bring the mixture to the boil. Stir in the salt and cayenne pepper and drop in the poached kefta. Cook over a high heat until almost all the liquid has evaporated. Carefully crack the eggs around the kefta, cover the tagine with a lid and leave the eggs to cook in the sauce and steam until they are just set. Sprinkle the roasted cumin and coarsely chopped parsley over the top of the dish. Serve immediately.

KEFTA TAGINE WITH LEMON

1 tablespoon olive oil

1 tablespoon butter or ghee

1 onion, roughly chopped

2–3 garlic cloves, halved and smashed

a thumb-sized piece of fresh ginger, peeled and finely chopped

1 red chilli/chile, deseeded and finely sliced

2 teaspoons ground turmeric

a small bunch of freshly chopped coriander/cilantro

juice of 1 lemon

1 lemon, cut into 6 segments, pips removed

a small bunch of fresh mint leaves, chopped

bread, buttered couscous or a salad, to serve

for the kefta

450 g/1 lb. finely minced/ground lamb

1 onion, finely chopped

a small bunch of fresh flat-leaf parsley, finely chopped

1–2 teaspoons ground cinnamon

1 teaspoon ground cumin

1 teaspoon ground coriander

½ teaspoon cayenne pepper or 1 teaspoon paprika

sea salt and freshly ground black pepper

serves 4–6

LIGHT AND LEMONY AND GIVEN A LOVELY YELLOW COLOUR BY THE TURMERIC, THIS KEFTA TAGINE IS QUITE DIFFERENT TO MANY OF THE SWEET AND SPICY TAGINES PREPARED WITH FRUIT. THE KEFTA CAN BE MADE AHEAD OF TIME AND KEPT IN THE FRIDGE UNTIL READY TO USE. SERVE THIS TAGINE WITH FRESH, CRUSTY BREAD, COUSCOUS OR A SIDE SALAD.

★ To make the kefta, pound the minced/ground lamb in a bowl with your hands by lifting it up and slapping it back down into the bowl to knock out the air. Add the onion, parsley and spices and season with salt and pepper. Again, using your hands, mix the ingredients together and knead well, pounding the mixture for a few minutes. Take pieces of the mixture and shape them into little walnut-sized balls. Set aside.

★ Heat the oil and butter in the base of a tagine or a heavy-based casserole. Stir in the onion, garlic, ginger and chilli/chile and sauté until they begin to brown. Add the turmeric and half the coriander/cilantro and pour in 300 ml/1¼ cups water. Bring to the boil, reduce the heat and simmer, covered, for 10 minutes.

★ Carefully place the kefta in the liquid, put the lid back on and poach them for about 15 minutes, rolling them in the liquid from time to time. Pour over the lemon juice, season the liquid with salt and pepper and tuck the lemon segments around the kefta. Cover and poach gently for a further 10 minutes. Sprinkle with the mint and the rest of the coriander/cilantro. Serve hot with bread, couscous or a salad.

MOROCCAN MEATBALL STEW

500 g/1 lb. 2 oz. minced/ground
lamb

1 onion, grated/minced

2 garlic cloves, finely chopped

a handful of fresh flat-leaf
parsley leaves, finely chopped

2 tablespoons olive oil

1 teaspoon ground cumin

1 teaspoon ground cinnamon

½ teaspoon cayenne pepper

400-g/14-oz. can chopped
tomatoes

a large handful of freshly
chopped coriander/cilantro
leaves

crunchy salad

1 small head of iceberg lettuce,
shredded into 2-cm/¾-inch-
wide strips

1 small red onion, very thinly
sliced

2 handfuls of fresh mint leaves

2 tablespoons olive oil

1 tablespoon freshly squeezed
lemon juice

sea salt and freshly ground black
pepper

serves 4

IF YOU ARE INTERESTED IN COOKING WITH SPICES, MOROCCAN FOOD IS
A GREAT PLACE TO START. THIS STYLE OF COOKING USES A RELATIVELY
SHORT LIST OF STAPLE SPICES, SUCH AS CUMIN, CINNAMON AND
CAYENNE PEPPER, BUT THEY ARE USED IN VARYING QUANTITIES TO
PRODUCE VERY DIFFERENT RESULTS FROM ONE RECIPE TO THE NEXT.
THIS VERSION OF A MOROCCAN STEW IS MADE IN A LARGE FRYING
PAN/SKILLET RATHER THAN THE TRADITIONAL TERRACOTTA POT. IT'S AN
IDEAL, FUSS-FREE ONE-POT DISH. THE JEWELLED RICE ON PAGE 138
WOULD MAKE A PERFECT ACCOMPANIMENT TO SERVE ALONGSIDE.

★ Put the minced/ground lamb, half the onion, half the garlic and the parsley
in a bowl. Use your hands to combine and throw the mixture against the side
of the bowl several times. Set aside.

★ Heat the oil in a large heavy-based frying pan/skillet set over a high heat
and cook the remaining onion and garlic for 5 minutes, until softened and
golden. Add the spices and cook, stirring constantly, for 1 minute, until
aromatic. Add the tomatoes and 250 ml/1 cup water and bring to the boil.
Cook for about 5 minutes.

★ With damp hands, roll the lamb mixture into walnut-sized balls and put
them directly into the sauce mixture as you do so. Reduce the heat, cover
and cook for about 15 minutes, until the meat is cooked through. Stir in the
coriander/cilantro and keep warm.

★ To make the salad, put the lettuce, onion and mint in a salad bowl and use
your hands to toss. Pour over the olive oil and lemon juice and season to taste
with salt and pepper. Serve the tagine with the crunchy salad on the side.

MOTHER-IN-LAW'S MEATBALLS

225 g /1¼ cups plus 1 tablespoon bulgur

225 g/8 oz. finely minced/ground lamb or beef

1–2 teaspoons very finely chopped dried red chilli/chile, or paprika

sea salt

plain/all-purpose flour, for coating

sunflower oil, for deep frying

a large bunch of fresh flat-leaf parsley

for the filling

1–2 tablespoons olive oil with a knob/pat of butter

1 onion, finely chopped

4 garlic cloves, finely chopped

60 g/½ cup walnuts, finely chopped

60 g/½ cup pistachios, finely chopped

1 teaspoon each ground cumin, ground coriander and dried thyme

120 g/4¼ oz. finely minced/ground beef or lamb

a small bunch of fresh flat-leaf parsley, finely chopped

sea salt and freshly ground black pepper

serves 4–6

IN THE ANATOLIAN REGION OF TURKEY, THIS TRADITIONAL DISH OF MEATBALLS FILLED WITH A MIXTURE OF NUTS AND HERBS, IS PREPARED FOR A NEW BRIDE BY HER MOTHER-IN-LAW. THE CAREFUL ACT OF MAKING, SEALING AND PRESENTING THESE STUFFED MEATBALLS, *İÇLİ KÖFTE*, IS TO SIGNIFY THAT THE LIPS OF THE NEW DAUGHTER-IN-LAW MUST NOW BE SEALED WITH DISCRETION.

★ Melt the olive oil and butter in a heavy-based saucepan and stir in the onion and garlic until they begin to colour. Add the walnuts and pistachios and stir for 1–2 minutes, then toss in the spices, thyme and minced/ground lamb and cook for 4–5 minutes, stirring occasionally. Stir in the parsley and season with salt and pepper. Leave the mixture to cool.

★ Meanwhile, put the bulgur into a bowl and pour in enough boiling water to just cover it. Cover the bowl and leave the bulgur to absorb the water for about 25 minutes. Squeeze the bulgur to make sure there is no excess water, then add the minced/ground lamb, finely chopped chilli/chile and season with salt. Using your hands, knead the ingredients together thoroughly.

★ Take a small portion of the mixture in the palm of a damp hand and mould it into a ball. Using a finger, hollow out an opening and put it on a flat surface. Repeat with the rest of the mixture.

★ Using a teaspoon, spoon a little filling into each hollow and pinch the edges together to seal. Gently squeeze the bulgur mixture together to form a ball, or a cone, and toss the balls in a little flour to lightly coat them.

★ Heat enough sunflower oil for deep-frying in a deep frying pan/skillet. Fry the meatballs in batches for 3–4 minutes, until golden brown. Drain on paper towels and serve hot on a bed of flat-leaf parsley to eat with them.

MEATBALLS IN AN EGG & LEMON SAUCE

MEATBALLS, IN THE FORM OF KOFTA (KEFTA) OR *'KIBBEH'*, ARE PERHAPS THE BEST KNOWN OF ALL MIDDLE EASTERN MEAT DISHES. THIS EGG AND LEMON SAUCE IS SOMETHING A BIT DIFFERENT THAT WORKS SO WELL.

meatballs

450 g/1 lb. finely minced/ground lean lamb

1 tablespoon medium or long-grain rice, washed and drained

a small bunch of fresh dill, finely chopped

a small bunch of fresh flat-leaf parsley, finely chopped

1–2 teaspoons sea salt

freshly ground black pepper

1–2 tablespoons plain/all-purpose flour

egg and lemon sauce

2 carrots, peeled and diced

1 small celeriac/celery root, peeled, trimmed and diced (kept in water with a squeeze of lemon juice to prevent it discolouring)

2 potatoes, peeled and diced

2 egg yolks

juice of 2 lemons

1 tablespoon plain, thick yogurt

1 teaspoon dried mint

a small bunch of fresh dill fronds, finely chopped

serves 4–6

★ Put the lamb into a bowl with the rice, dill, parsley, salt and a good grinding of black pepper. Knead the mixture for about 5 minutes, until well combined, and slap the mixture down into the bottom of the bowl to knock out the air.

★ Take small portions of the mixture into the palm of a damp hand and mould them into tight, cherry-sized balls. Spoon the flour onto a flat surface and roll the balls in it until lightly coated. Put them aside.

★ Pour 1 litre/quart water into a heavy-based shallow saucepan and bring to the boil. Add the carrots and celeriac/celery root, drained of the lemon water, and cook the vegetables for about 5 minutes. Keep the water boiling and drop in the meatballs. Reduce the heat, cover the saucepan and simmer for about 15 minutes. Add the potatoes and simmer, uncovered, for a further 15–20 minutes.

★ In a bowl, beat the egg yolks with the lemon juice, yogurt and mint. Spoon a little of the cooking liquid into the mixture then tip it all into the pan, stirring all the time, until it is heated through and the sauce has thickened. Be careful not to bring the liquid to the boil. Serve the meatballs directly from the saucepan into shallow bowls and spoon the sauce around them. Garnish with the dill and serve with fresh bread or plain rice to mop up the sauce.

CURRIED LAMB BALLS

AN INDIAN TWIST ON THE CLASSIC MEATBALL. IN THIS RECIPE THE MEAT IS COMBINED WITH FRAGRANT HERBS AND SPICES AND SIMMERED SLOWLY IN A SPICY TOMATO SAUCE. GREAT AS A MID-WEEK SUPPER WHEN SERVED WITH WARM NAAN OR BASMATI RICE.

3 tablespoons sunflower oil

1 onion, finely chopped

2 tablespoons medium curry paste

400-g/14-oz. can chopped tomatoes

200 ml/generous ¾ cup chicken stock

150 ml/⅔ cup double/heavy cream

meatballs

2 teaspoons finely grated/minced root ginger

4 teaspoons crushed garlic

1 teaspoon ground cinnamon

a large handful of freshly chopped coriander/cilantro leaves, plus extra to garnish

800 g/1¾ lbs. minced/ground lamb

serves 4

★ To make the meatballs, put the ginger, garlic, cinnamon, coriander/ cilantro and minced/ground meat in a mixing bowl. Season well and, using your fingers, mix well to combine. Roll tablespoons of the mixture into bite-sized balls, place on a tray, cover and chill in the fridge for 1–2 hours.

★ Heat 2 tablespoons of the sunflower oil in a large, non-stick frying pan/ skillet, then add the meatballs and cook in batches until lightly browned. Remove with a slotted spoon and set aside.

★ Add the remaining oil to the pan and place over a medium heat. Add the onion and stir-fry for 4–5 minutes, then stir in the curry paste. Stir-fry for 1–2 minutes, then add the canned tomatoes and stock. Bring to the boil, reduce the heat and leave to simmer gently, uncovered, for 10–15 minutes.

★ Add the meatballs to the pan and stir carefully to coat them in the sauce. Simmer gently for 10–15 minutes, or until cooked through. Stir in the cream and cook for a final 2–3 minutes. Remove from the heat and garnish with the extra coriander/cilantro leaves. Serve with warm naan or steamed basmati rice.

CHAPTER 4

POULTRY

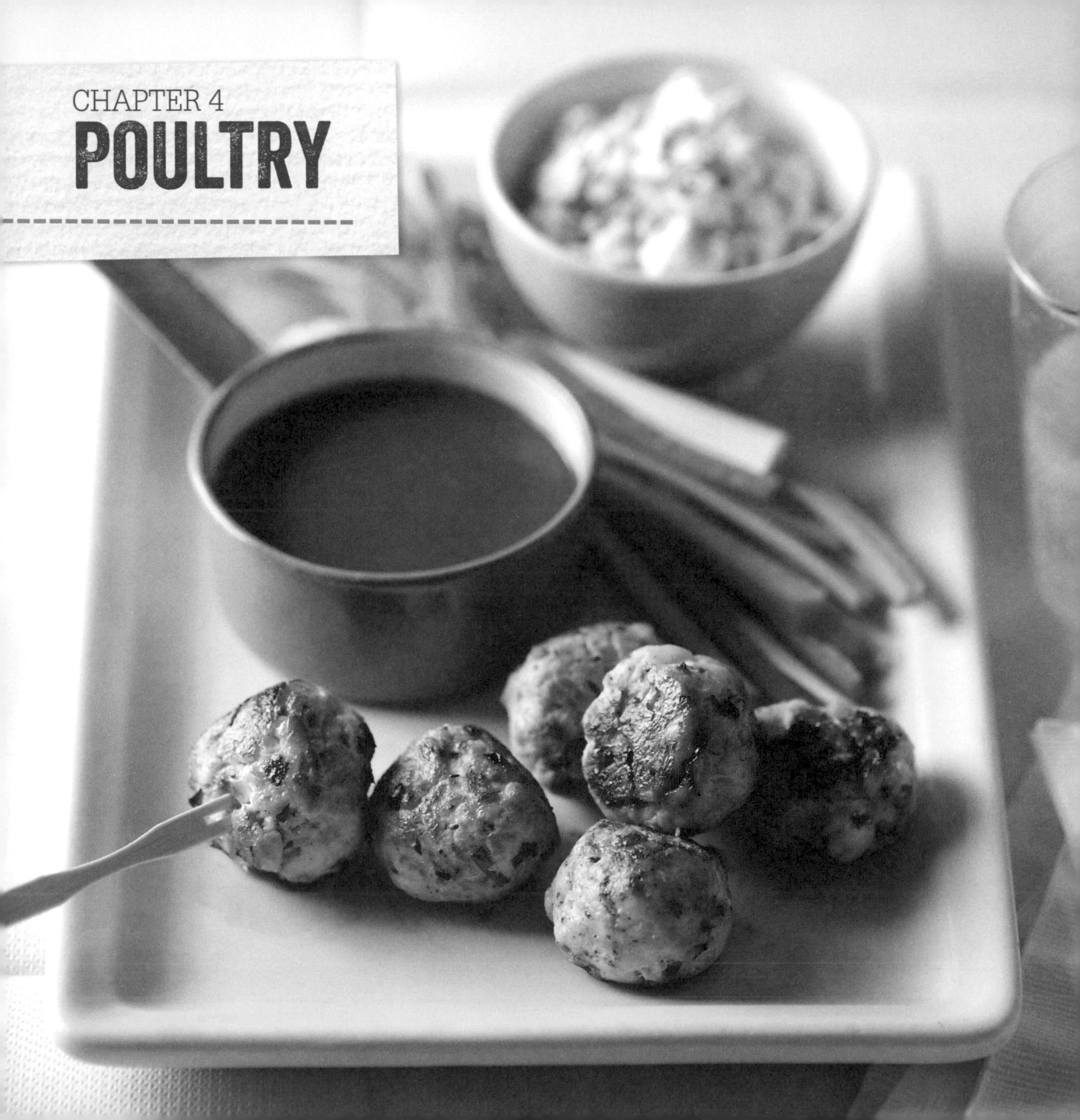

BUFFALO CHICKEN BALLS

meatballs

500 g/1 lb. 2 oz. chicken breast fillets

1 small onion, grated/minced

2 garlic cloves, crushed

a small bunch of fresh flat-leaf parsley, chopped

salt and freshly ground black pepper

a little olive oil, for drizzling

buffalo sauce

25 g/2 tablespoons butter

150 ml/⅔ cup Frank's Hot Sauce or other hot sauce

blue cheese dip

150 g/⅔ cup mayonnaise

2 tablespoons sour cream

75 g/⅔ cup blue cheese, crumbled

1 small celery stick, finely chopped

freshly chopped flat-leaf parsley

to serve

celery sticks

carrot sticks

2 baking sheets, greased

makes 16

THESE ARE VERY POPULAR IN THE USA WHERE THEY ARE SERVED AS A SNACK AT PARTIES OR SPORTING EVENTS. QUICK AND EASY TO MAKE, THEY ARE OVEN BAKED AND THEN ADDED TO A DELICIOUS HOT SAUCE AND SERVED ALONGSIDE A COOLING BLUE CHEESE DIP.

★ Preheat the oven to 180°C (350°F) Gas 4.

★ Chop the chicken breast fillets very finely or blend in a food processor for a few seconds.

★ Put all the meatball ingredients together in a large bowl and mix together until well combined. The mixture will be quite sticky. With damp hands, shape the mixture into 16 small balls. Arrange the balls on the baking sheets. Spray or drizzle with a little olive oil. Bake for 10–15 minutes, turning them once during cooking time to brown the balls evenly.

★ While the balls are baking, make the buffalo sauce by melting the butter in a large frying pan/skillet. Stir in the Frank's Hot Sauce or other hot sauce, mixing well to combine. Heat the sauce thoroughly.

★ Spoon the baked meatballs into the sauce, turning them over several times to coat evenly with the mixture. Transfer the meatballs to a serving platter. Pour any remaining hot sauce into a serving bowl.

★ To make the blue cheese dip, mix together the mayonnaise, sour cream, cheese and celery (reserving a little for garnish) until well blended and creamy. Spoon into a serving bowl and garnish with the remaining celery and a little chopped parsley.

★ Serve the meatballs with the buffalo sauce, blue cheese dip, celery and carrot sticks.

CHRISTMAS TURKEY MEATBALLS

CRAMMED WITH CHRISTMAS FLAVOURS AND COLOURS, THESE LITTLE MORSELS ARE GREAT SERVED HOT OR COLD AS A FESTIVE SNACK OR CANAPÉ. THEY ARE DELICIOUS WITH THE TANGY CRANBERRY DIP.

meatballs

50 g/scant ⅓ cup pine nuts

450 g/1 lb. raw turkey breast meat

50 g/1 cup fresh breadcrumbs

1 small onion, finely chopped

25 g/1 cup spinach, finely chopped

50 g/scant ⅓ cup dried cranberries, roughly chopped

30 g/½ cup Parmesan cheese, finely grated

15 g/½ cup fresh sage, finely chopped or 2 teaspoons dried sage

1 egg, beaten

2 tablespoons whole milk

sea salt and freshly ground black pepper

cranberry dip

225 g/2¼ cups fresh or frozen cranberries

150 g/¾ cup caster/granulated sugar

1 tablespoon balsamic vinegar

2 baking sheets, lined with baking parchment

makes 24

★ Heat a small frying pan/skillet over a medium heat. Add the pine nuts and cook for a few minutes until aromatic and light brown.

★ Chop the turkey meat very finely or process in a food processor for a few seconds until fairly smooth but still with some texture.

★ Place the turkey, pine nuts and the remaining meatball ingredients into a large bowl and mix with your hands until thoroughly combined. Cover the bowl and chill in the fridge for 30 minutes.

★ Preheat the oven to 200°C (400°F) Gas 6.

★ With wet hands, shape the mixture into 24 bite-sized balls, arranging them 2.5 cm/1 inch apart on the baking sheets. Bake for approximately 10–15 minutes until the balls are golden brown and springy to the touch.

★ To make the cranberry dip, combine the ingredients in a small saucepan with 100 ml/7 tablespoons water. Bring to the boil, reduce the heat to simmer and cook, uncovered for 20–30 minutes until thick and syrupy.

CHICKEN MEATBALLS WITH ROASTED VEGETABLES

THESE UNUSUAL MEATBALLS REQUIRE SOMETHING MORE EXOTIC THAN TOMATO SAUCE, HENCE THE ROASTED TOMATOES AND ONIONS, WHICH WORK A TREAT. SERVE WITH A CRISP GREEN SIDE SALAD.

3 onions

6 fresh plum tomatoes, cored and quartered

4 tablespoons olive oil

1 teaspoon dried thyme

125 g/2 cups mushrooms, coarsely chopped

100 g/3½ oz. pancetta or ham

a large handful of fresh flat-leaf parsley leaves, chopped

2 garlic cloves, crushed

500 g/1 lb. 2 oz. minced/ground chicken

1 teaspoon paprika

1 egg, beaten

5 tablespoons fresh breadcrumbs

whole milk, to soften

sea salt and freshly ground black pepper

2 baking sheets, 1 lined with foil, the other with baking parchment

serves 4–6

★ Preheat the oven to 200°C (400°F) Gas 6.

★ Halve one of the onions, chop coarsely and set aside. Cut the remaining onions into quarters and toss with 2–3 tablespoons of the oil and the thyme. Arrange on the foil-lined baking sheet with the tomatoes. Set aside while you prepare the meatballs.

★ In a small food processor, combine the chopped onion, mushrooms pancetta and parsley. Process until finely chopped. Transfer to a frying pan/ skillet, add 1–2 tablespoons of the oil and cook for 3–5 minutes until softened. Add the garlic, season well and cook for 1 minute more. Let cool slightly.

★ In a bowl, combine the chicken, paprika, egg, breadcrumbs and the cooled mushroom mixture. Add a good pinch of salt. Mix well with your hands to combine. Take a small pinch of the mixture and cook it in the frying pan/skillet used to cook the mushroom mixture. When cooked, taste it and adjust the seasoning as necessary. The mixture should be quite moist and it will be possible – if difficult – to form the mixture into balls. If it is too dry, soften with milk, adding 1 tablespoon at a time.

★ Shape the chicken mixture into walnut-sized balls and arrange them on the paper-lined baking sheet. Season the onions and tomatoes and put both baking sheets into the preheated oven. Bake for about 35–45 minutes, until the meatballs and vegetables are browned. Serve together.

PANCETTA & CHICKEN MEATBALLS

500 g/1 lb. 2 oz. minced/ground chicken

50 g/1¾ oz. thinly sliced pancetta or bacon, coarsely chopped

6 spring onions/scallions, finely chopped

4 garlic cloves, finely chopped

2 red chillies/chiles, deseeded and finely chopped

4 tablespoons freshly grated Parmesan cheese, plus extra to serve

1 tablespoon fresh thyme leaves

1 tablespoon olive oil

200 ml/¾ cup red wine

2 x 400-g/14-oz. cans plum tomatoes

a pinch of caster/granulated sugar

300 g/10⅓ oz. dried pasta, such as gnocchi or conchiglie

sea salt and freshly ground black pepper

serves 4

MEATBALLS ARE A TIME-HONOURED ACCOMPANIMENT TO PASTA. THESE TASTY LITTLE MOUTHFULS ARE MADE WITH CHICKEN, PANCETTA AND HERBS, SO ARE SOMEWHAT LIGHTER THAN THE TRADITIONAL BEEF OR PORK VARIATIONS, BUT JUST AS COMFORTING.

★ Put the minced/ground chicken, pancetta, spring onions/scallions, garlic, chilli/chile, Parmesan cheese and thyme into a bowl. Add plenty of salt and pepper and mix well. Using damp hands, shape the mixture into 24 small, firm balls.

★ Heat the oil in a large saucepan, add the meatballs and cook for about 5 minutes, turning them frequently until browned all over. Add the wine and simmer vigorously for 1–2 minutes.

★ Add the tomatoes, breaking them up with a wooden spoon. Stir in the sugar, and add salt and pepper to taste. Bring to the boil, then simmer very gently, uncovered, for 30 minutes until the sauce is rich and thickened.

★ Meanwhile, bring a large saucepan of water to the boil. Add a good pinch of salt, then the pasta, and cook until al dente, or according to the timings on the packet.

★ Drain the pasta well and return it to the warm saucepan. Add the meatballs and sauce to the pasta, toss well to mix, then divide between 4 bowls. Serve topped with extra Parmesan cheese.

JEWISH MOTHER'S CHICKEN SOUP

PERHAPS THE MOST FAMOUS OF ALL CHICKEN SOUPS, THIS IS GENERALLY SAID TO CURE ALL KNOWN AILMENTS. IT IS INFINITELY CHEERING, SO DO GO TO THE EFFORT OF MAKING IT EVERY NOW AND THEN. FOR THE BEST FLAVOUR, USE A WHOLE BIRD, CUT UP OR JUST THE WINGS AND BACKS, WHICH ARE RICH IN THE GELATIN THAT GIVES THIS SOUP ITS BODY.

1 kg/2 lbs. 3 oz. chicken pieces, such as backs and wings, chopped

1 onion, quartered

1 carrot, quartered

1 celery rib/stalk, quartered

2 garlic cloves, crushed but whole

1 fresh bouquet garni (a bunch of herbs such as thyme, bay and parsley, tied with string)

2 teaspoons black peppercorns

sea salt

to serve

250 g/9 oz. shredded cooked chicken

4 tablespoons freshly chopped flat-leaf parsley and/or dill (optional)

matzoh balls (optional) (see method)

serves 4

★ Put all the ingredients except the salt into a large saucepan or stockpot with 2 litres/quarts cold water. Bring to the boil. Skim off and discard the foam that rises to the surface. Reduce the heat to a simmer. Part-cover and cook for 1½–2 hours. Add salt to taste.

★ Strain through a sieve/strainer. For a clearer stock, line the sieve/strainer with wet muslin/cheesecloth or wet paper towels. Remove the flesh from the bones, shred it and reserve, covered. Discard the skin and bones.

★ To remove fat from the stock, let the stock cool a little, then trail torn paper towel edges across the surface. Alternatively, chill the stock (preferably overnight), then remove the thin film of solidified fat with a slotted spoon.

★ Return the stock to a clean saucepan, add the shredded chicken, bring to the boil and reheat.

★ Serve the soup with matzoh balls and chopped herbs, if desired.

Note: To make matzoh balls, put 50 g/1¾ oz. medium matzoh meal in a bowl with 1 beaten egg, 2 tablespoons warm water and ½ teaspoon salt. Stir well, then chill in the fridge for 20 minutes to firm up. Wet your hands, take pieces of dough the size of a marble and roll into balls. You should have about 16–24. Poach them in a large saucepan of boiling salted water for 5 minutes. Remove with a slotted spoon, put on a plate, cover and set aside. To serve, reheat in the salted water, drain, then add to the hot soup.

JAPANESE TSUKUNE CHICKEN MEATBALLS

yakitori sauce

120 ml/½ cup mirin

120 ml/½ cup soy sauce

50 ml/3 tablespoons sake

25 g/2 tablespoons dark brown sugar

1 tablespoon sherry vinegar

2 garlic cloves, crushed

3 spring onions/scallions, finely chopped

5-cm/2-inch piece fresh ginger, peeled and grated

10 black peppercorns

meatballs

750 g/1⅔ lbs. chicken thigh meat

50 g/⅔ cup panko breadcrumbs

2 spring onions/scallions, finely chopped

2.5-cm/1-inch piece fresh ginger, peeled and grated

2 garlic cloves, crushed

1 egg, beaten

1 teaspoon toasted sesame oil

1 teaspoon salt

freshly ground black pepper

8 wooden skewers, soaked in water 30 minutes before use

makes 24

TSUKUNE ARE STICKY GLAZED CHICKEN MEATBALLS COOKED ON WOODEN SKEWERS OVER A SPECIAL CHARCOAL GRILL IN JAPANESE *YAKITORI* RESTAURANTS. THEY ARE USUALLY SERVED WITH A YAKITORI SAUCE.

★ For the Yakitori sauce, put all the ingredients in a medium saucepan. Stir well, bring to the boil over a high heat, reduce the heat to a simmer then cook for approximately 40–45 minutes or until the mixture is thick and syrupy, stirring occasionally. Strain then store in the fridge until required. The sauce will become thicker when cold.

★ For the meatballs, chop the chicken meat very finely or process in a food processor until fairly smooth. Transfer to a large bowl. Add all the remaining meatball ingredients and stir in one direction until everything is very well combined, smooth in texture and pale in colour. The mixture should be very thoroughly mixed to prevent the meatballs from falling apart during cooking.

★ With damp hands, shape the mixture into 24 balls about 5 cm/2 inches in diameter. Arrange the balls on a plate or baking sheet lined with baking parchment, cover lightly with clingfilm/plastic wrap and chill in the fridge for 30 minutes.

★ Thread three balls onto each of the wooden skewers and arrange on a lightly oiled baking sheet which can fit under the grill/broiler.

★ Preheat the grill/broiler to medium. Grill/broil the balls for 6–8 minutes until well browned, then carefully rotate the skewers and cook on the second side for 5–6 minutes. Turn the skewers again several times, cooking for a few minutes each time until the balls are fully and evenly cooked. Brush the Yakitori sauce over the meatballs and cook for 2–3 minutes longer. Repeat several times until all the balls are glossy and sticky. Transfer the skewers to a serving plate, brush with extra sauce and allow to rest for 5 minutes. Serve with any remaining sauce.

THAI CHICKEN MEATBALLS

MILDLY SPICY AND FULL OF FLAVOUR, THESE CHICKEN BALLS ARE SHAPED WITH YOUR HANDS, THEN SIMPLY BAKED IN THE OVEN – NO FRYING IS NEEDED. SERVE AS PARTY BITES OR AS A MAIN WITH THAI FRAGRANT RICE AND EXTRA SWEET CHILLI/CHILE SAUCE (IT'S MILD, NOT HOT – A BIT LIKE THAI TOMATO KETCHUP), FOR DIPPING.

50 g/1¾ oz. fresh bread (about 2 medium slices)

500 g/1 lb. 2 oz. minced/ground chicken or turkey

1 egg

2 spring onions/scallions

½ teaspoon ground coriander

a small bunch of fresh coriander/cilantro leaves

1 teaspoon fish sauce or soy sauce

2 teaspoons sweet chilli/chile sauce (page 131), plus extra for serving

a large baking dish, greased with vegetable oil

makes 12

★ Preheat the oven to 200°C (400°F) Gas 6.

★ Tear up the bread and put it into a blender or processor. Process the bread until it turns into crumbs. Tip the crumbs into a bowl. Add the minced chicken or turkey. Crack the egg into the bowl.

★ Rinse the spring onions/scallions. Using a small knife, cut off the hairy root ends and the very dark leaves at the top. Cut the onions into very thin slices. Add to the bowl, then add the ground coriander. Snip the fresh coriander/cilantro leaves straight into the bowl. Add the fish sauce or soy sauce and the sweet chilli/chile sauce to the bowl. Using damp hands, mix well to combine and shape into small balls – use about 1 tablespoon of mixture for each.

★ Rub the base of a large baking dish with oil, then arrange the balls in the dish. Put it into the preheated oven to bake for 25 minutes until golden brown and cooked all the way through.

★ Serve the meatballs straight from the baking dish with Thai fragrant rice and extra sweet chilli/chile sauce in a small bowl for dipping.

chicken balls

2 eggs

1 teaspoon salt

ground white pepper, to taste

1 litre/quart peanut oil, for frying

40 g/⅓ cup cornflour/cornstarch, plus 1 tablespoon for thickening

35 g/¼ cup plain/all-purpose flour

4 rings fresh (or canned) pineapple, drained (juice reserved)

675 g/1½ lbs. boneless skinless chicken, chopped into bite-sized pieces

1 tablespoon fresh ginger, minced

1 teaspoon garlic, minced

2 green (bell) peppers, in small pieces

½ tablespoon dried chilli/hot red pepper flakes

¼ cup chopped spring onion/scallion

1 tablespoon rice wine

sweet and sour sauce

1 tablespoon soy sauce

3½ tablespoons sugar

3½ tablespoons white vinegar

zest of 1 orange

serves 4

SWEET & SOUR CHICKEN BALLS

THIS DISH COMBINES TWO DELICIOUS DISHES THAT ARE JUST TOO HARD TO CHOOSE BETWEEN IN A CHINESE RESTAURANT!

★ To make the sweet and sour sauce, mix all the ingredients together and 1 tablespoon water in a mixing bowl. Transfer to a small saucepan and bring to the boil, then remove from the heat.

★ For the chicken, in a large bowl, stir together the eggs, salt, pepper and 1 tablespoon of the peanut oil. Mix well. In a small bowl, whisk 40 g/⅓ cup cornflour/cornstarch and flour together. Mix the flour mixture into the egg mixture. Add the chicken pieces, tossing to coat.

★ Heat the rest of the peanut oil in a large frying pan/skillet, wok or deep-fat fryer to 190°C (375°F) or until the oil is bubbling steadily. Add the coated chicken pieces, a few at a time. Fry for 3–4 minutes or until golden crisp. Remove the chicken with a slotted spoon, drain on paper towels then set aside.

★ Clean the wok or frying pan/skillet and heat for 15 seconds over a high heat. Add a little oil and then add the ginger and garlic. Stir-fry for 10 seconds. Add the peppers, chilli/hot red pepper flakes, spring onions/scallions and rice wine. Stir for a few seconds. Add the sweet and sour sauce and bring to the boil. Add the cooked chicken, stirring until mixed together well.

★ Stir 60 ml/¼ cup water into the remaining 1 tablespoon cornflour/cornstarch until smooth and add to the chicken. Heat until the sauce has thickened and then serve at once.

CRISPY DUCK BONBONS

- -

THESE DELICIOUS BONBONS ARE IDEAL FOR A LIGHT LUNCH WITH A BRIGHT ASIAN-STYLE SALAD OR AS A DINNER PARTY APPETIZER.

2 duck legs, each weighing approx. 225 g/8 oz.

800 g/1¾ lbs. (about 4 large) potatoes, peeled and cut into cubes

2 teaspoons freshly chopped thyme

1 egg yolk

50 g/⅓ cup plain/all-purpose flour

sea salt and freshly ground black pepper

to coat

3 eggs

2 tablespoons whole milk

200 g/3½ cups fresh breadcrumbs

to serve

hoisin sauce, for dipping

a roasting pan, fitted with a wire rack

a deep-fat fryer

makes 18

★ Preheat the oven to 190°C (375°F) Gas 5.

★ Put the duck legs on the wire rack and prick the skin. Roast for 70–90 minutes in the preheated oven until fully cooked. Cool slightly, remove the skin and discard, then cut the meat from the bones. Shred or roughly chop the meat.

★ Cook the potatoes in plenty of boiling salted water or steam until tender. Drain and mash until smooth. Transfer to a large bowl.

★ Add the duck meat, thyme, egg yolk and seasoning. Mix together until thoroughly combined. Divide the mixture into 18 golf-ball-sized balls and lightly dust each with flour, shaking off the excess.

★ Beat the eggs with the milk in a bowl. Put the breadcrumbs on a plate. Dip each ball in the egg mixture then coat with the breadcrumbs. Repeat the process once more so the balls are coated twice. Put the balls on a plate and chill in the fridge for 30 minutes.

★ Preheat the deep-fat fryer to 140°C (275°F).

★ Fry the balls in batches for 4–5 minutes until golden brown. Drain on paper towels. Serve with hoisin sauce as a dip.

MINI FISH KEFTA WITH SAFFRON & LEMON

- -

450 g/1 lb. white fish fillets, such as sea bass or haddock, skinned and flaked

1–2 teaspoons harissa paste

rind of ½ preserved lemon, finely chopped

a small bunch of fresh coriander/cilantro, chopped

a pinch of saffron fronds, soaked in 1 teaspoon water to draw out the colour

2 teaspoons runny honey

1 egg

2 slices Moroccan or rustic bread, with crusts removed and bread ground into crumbs

2 tablespoons plain/all-purpose flour

sunflower oil, for frying

sea salt and freshly ground black pepper

1 lemon, cut into wedges, to serve

serves 4

ONE OF THE JOYS OF THE STREET FOOD IN MOROCCAN COASTAL TOWNS, SUCH AS ESSAOUIRA, IS THE AROMA OF GRILLED OR FRIED FISH COOKING WITH SPICES AND CORIANDER/CILANTRO AS THE FISH KEFTA ARE PREPARED FOR PASSERS-BY. MINI FISH KEFTA ARE OFTEN SERVED AS AN APPETIZER ACCOMPANIED BY LEMON WEDGES, SALAD, A SELECTION OF DIPS AND A BOWL OF OLIVES.

★ Put the fish in a bowl and add the harissa paste, preserved lemon, coriander/cilantro, saffron and honey. Beat in the egg, season with salt and pepper, and add enough breadcrumbs to bind the mixture. Knead the mixture with damp hands and take small apricot-sized lumps into your palms to mould into small balls. Roll the balls lightly in the flour.

★ Heat the oil in a heavy-based frying pan/skillet and fry the balls in batches for 3–4 minutes, until golden brown all over. Drain them on paper towels and serve hot with lemon wedges to squeeze over them.

TURMERIC FISH BALLS WITH SUNFLOWER SEEDS

2 tablespoons sunflower seeds (reserve a few for garnishing)

450 g/1 lb. fresh white fish fillets, such as haddock or sea bass

2 slices day-old bread, soaked in a little water and squeezed dry

1 red onion, finely chopped

2 garlic cloves, crushed

1 green or red chilli/chile, stalk and seeds removed, and finely chopped

1 teaspoon ground cumin

1–2 teaspoons ground turmeric

a small bunch of fresh flat-leaf parsley, finely chopped

a small bunch of fresh coriander/cilantro, finely chopped (reserve a little for garnishing)

1 egg, lightly beaten

sea salt and freshly ground black pepper

3–4 tablespoons plain/all-purpose flour

2 tablespoons olive oil with a knob/pat of butter

a bunch of rocket/arugula leaves, rinsed and drained

1–2 limes or lemons, cut into wedges

serves 4–6

THESE MEZZE-STYLE FISH BALLS ARE EASY TO MAKE AND VERY VERSATILE. ALMOST ANY FRESH FISH CAN BE SUBSTITUTED, OR EVEN CANS OF COOKED TUNA. FISH CAN STAND UP TO THE TYPICALLY STRONG FLAVOURS USUALLY FOUND IN MIDDLE EASTERN-CUISINE. THESE BEAUTIFUL BALLS ARE STUFFED WITH CHILLIES/CHILES, CUMIN, TURMERIC, SAFFRON AND CINNAMON, AND LOTS OF FRESH HERBS.

★ First, dry roast the sunflower seeds. Heat a small, heavy-based frying pan/skillet and toss in the sunflower seeds for 1–2 minutes, until they brown a little and emit a nutty aroma. Tip them onto a plate and put aside.

★ In a bowl, break up the fish fillets with a fork. Add the bread, onion, garlic, chilli/chile, cumin, turmeric and most of the sunflower seeds. Toss in the fresh herbs and mix well with the beaten egg.

★ Using damp hands, mould portions of the mixture into small apricot-sized balls. Toss them in the flour.

★ Heat the olive oil and butter in a wide shallow frying pan/skillet and fry the fish balls in batches until golden on both sides. Drain on paper towels.

★ Arrange the rocket/arugula leaves and fish balls on a dish, or wrap a leaf around each fish ball. Garnish with the reserved sprinkling of sunflower seeds and the reserved coriander/cilantro and serve with wedges of lime or lemon to squeeze over them.

SALT COD *ALBÓNDIGAS*

125 g/4½ oz. salt cod

300 g/10½ oz. potatoes

1 bay leaf

1 garlic clove, crushed

1 tablespoon freshly chopped flat-leaf parsley

freshly ground white pepper

1 egg

plain/all-purpose flour, for dusting

oil, for frying

Fresh Aïoli (page 130), to serve

a deep-fat fryer

serves 4

DRIED SALT COD IS KNOWN AS *BACALAO* IN SPAIN. IT CAN BE BOUGHT ONLINE OR IN SPANISH DELIS AS WELL AS CARIBBEAN AND ITALIAN STORES. ALTHOUGH FRESH FISH OF ALL KINDS ARE WIDELY AVAILABLE IN SPAIN, SALT COD HAS A LOVELY UNIQUE FLAVOUR AND AN ALMOST RELIGIOUS SIGNIFICANCE. IF YOU FIND IT HARD TO BUY, SUBSTITUTE WITH ANOTHER MEATY WHITE FISH AND HALVE THE COOKING TIME.

★ Put the cod in a bowl, cover with cold water and keep in the fridge for at least 24 hours, changing the water every 6 hours.

★ Prick the potatoes with a skewer, then bake in a preheated oven at 200°C (400°F) Gas 6 for 1 hour or until soft on the inside. Remove from the oven, scoop the flesh out of the skins into a bowl and mash.

★ Put the cod in a saucepan, cover with cold water, add the bay leaf, bring to the boil and simmer for 30 minutes. Remove from the heat and let cool. Remove the skin and flake the flesh into a bowl, making sure to remove all the bones. Add the flesh to the mashed potatoes, then stir in the garlic, parsley, pepper and 2 tablespoons of the cod cooking liquid. Roll the mixture into balls about the size of a walnut. Put in a bowl, cover with clingfilm/plastic wrap and chill in the fridge for 2–3 hours to firm up.

★ Put the egg in a bowl, add 1 tablespoon water and beat lightly. Put the flour on a plate. Dip the cod balls in the egg, then roll in the flour.

★ Fill a deep-fat fryer with oil to the manufacturer's recommended level and heat to 195°C (380°F). Cook the balls, in batches if necessary, for about 3 minutes or until golden brown. Remove with a slotted spoon and drain on paper towels. Serve hot with Fresh Aïoli.

ITALIAN SWORDFISH BALLS

350 g/12½ oz. swordfish, skinned, boned and cut into cubes

100 g/3½ oz. stale bread (about 2 slices), crumbled

1 onion, coarsely grated/minced

4 tablespoons capers, drained and chopped

1 tablespoon drained and chopped gherkins/pickles (cornichons)

juice of 1 lemon

1 teaspoon freshly ground white pepper

8 canned anchovies, drained and mashed to a pulp

90 ml/generous ⅓ cup extra virgin olive oil

2 tablespoons pine nuts

freshly grated zest and juice of 1 orange

a large handful of freshly chopped flat-leaf parsley

flatbread or crusty bread, to serve

serves 4–6

THESE TINY BALLS OF MINCED MEATY SWORDFISH, WITH BREAD, HERBS AND TYPICALLY ITALIAN SEASONINGS, ARE PAN-FRIED THEN SERVED WITH TOASTED PINE NUTS AND AN ORANGE, ANCHOVY AND PARSLEY SAUCE. YOU COULD SUBSTITUTE HALIBUT, MONKFISH OR ANY OTHER MEATY FISH.

★ Put the fish, bread, onion, capers, gherkins/pickles, lemon juice, pepper and half the anchovies in a food processor. Pulse in brief bursts to a soft, dense paste, but don't over-process. Transfer to a work surface and take heaped teaspoons of the mixture, squeeze them to make firm, then roll each portion into a neat ball. You should have 36, about 3 cm/1¼ inches in diameter.

★ Put half the oil in a frying pan/skillet, preferably non-stick, and heat until very hot. Add half the fish balls, and shake the pan over a medium heat for 3–4 minutes, so the balls roll and turn and brown all over. Test one: it should feel dense and firm and be the same colour right through. Remove the balls from the pan and keep hot on a plate. Add the remaining oil to the pan and cook the remaining balls in the same way.

★ Pour all but 4 tablespoons of the oil out of the pan. Add the pine nuts and shake and stir until golden brown, then remove with a slotted spoon. Keep hot with the fish balls.

★ Add the orange zest and juice and remaining anchovies to the pan. Stir over a medium heat until syrupy. Add half the parsley and extra lemon juice, if necessary.

★ Serve the fish balls hot, warm or cool with the sauce. Sprinkle with the remaining parsley and serve with crusty bread or a crisp Italian flatbread.

THAI SALMON BALLS

450 /1 lb. salmon fillets, skinned and finely chopped

2 teaspoons lemon grass paste

1 red chilli/chile, deseeded and finely chopped

2 spring onions/scallions, finely chopped

grated zest of 1 lime

25 g/½ cup fresh coriander/cilantro, finely chopped

1 tablespoon Thai fish sauce

2 tablespoons plain/all-purpose flour, for dusting

2 tablespoons vegetable oil, for frying

lemon wedges, to serve

ginger and miso dipping sauce

60 g/4 tablespoons miso paste

60 ml/4 tablespoons rice wine vinegar

juice of 1 lime

5-cm/2-inch piece fresh ginger, peeled and grated

1 teaspoon caster/granulated sugar

makes 12

SALMON IS SUCH A POPULAR CHOICE OF FISH, AND THESE AROMATIC THAI SALMON BALLS ARE IDEAL FOR SHARING WITH FRIENDS. THEY ARE FULL OF FAMILIAR TANGY FRESH THAI FLAVOURS: LEMONGRASS, LIME AND THAI FISH SAUCE. THEY FIND A PERFECT PARTNER WITH THE RICH SWEET HEAT OF THE GINGER AND MISO DIPPING SAUCE.

★ Put the salmon, lemon grass paste, chilli/chile, spring onions/scallions, lime zest and coriander/cilantro into a large bowl. Add the fish sauce and mix together until thoroughly combined.

★ With damp hands, divide the mixture into 12 pieces. Roll each one into a ball and then flatten slightly. Dip each in the flour, shaking off the excess. Arrange the balls on a baking sheet lined with baking parchment and cover loosely with clingfilm/plastic wrap. Chill in the fridge for 1 hour.

★ Heat the oil in a large heavy-based frying pan/skillet and when very hot fry the fish balls for 2–3 minutes on each side until golden brown. Lift out and drain on paper towels.

★ For the ginger and miso dipping sauce, place the miso paste into a small bowl. Whisk in a little of the rice vinegar to make a smooth paste, then add the remaining rice vinegar, lime juice, ginger and sugar, whisking well to combine.

★ Serve the fish balls with the dipping sauce and with lemon wedges to squeeze over them.

CHINESE SHRIMP BALLS

----

prawn/shrimp balls

450 g/1 lb. raw prawns/shrimp, shelled, deveined and chopped

2.5-cm/1-inch piece fresh ginger, peeled and grated

2 garlic cloves, crushed

1 red chilli/chile, deseeded and finely chopped

2 teaspoons light soy sauce

1 teaspoon toasted sesame oil

25 g/½ cup fresh coriander/cilantro, finely chopped

2 spring onions/scallions, finely chopped

1 teaspoon caster/granulated sugar

1 tablespoon cornflour/cornstarch

soy and sesame dipping sauce

1 tablespoon olive oil

2 garlic cloves, crushed

½ teaspoon dried chilli/hot red pepper flakes

1 tablespoon sesame seeds

2.5-cm/1-inch piece fresh ginger, peeled and grated

2 tablespoons light soy sauce

1 tablespoon runny honey

1 tablespoon sesame oil

grated zest and juice of 1 small lime, plus lime wedges, to serve

a deep-fat fryer

makes 18

AN AUTHENTIC TASTE OF CHINA, THESE LITTLE PRAWN/SHRIMP BALLS WITH DELICATE FLAVOURS ARE A REAL CROWD PLEASER. GREAT SERVED AS AN APPETIZER WITH SOY AND SESAME DIPPING SAUCE AND A SQUEEZE OF LIME OR AS PART OF A MAIN MEAL WITH RICE.

★ Put all the prawn/shrimp ball ingredients in a large bowl and mix together with your hands until thoroughly combined.

★ With wet hands, shape the mixture into 18 bite-sized balls. Arrange the balls on a plate or baking sheet lined with baking parchment. Cover lightly with clingfilm/plastic wrap and chill in the fridge for 30 minutes.

★ Preheat the deep-fat fryer to 180°C (350°F).

★ Deep-fry the prawn/shrimp balls a few at a time for 2–3 minutes until golden brown. Drain on paper towels.

★ For the soy and sesame dipping sauce, heat the oil in a heavy-based frying pan/skillet. Add the garlic, chilli/hot red pepper flakes and sesame seeds and cook gently for 2–3 minutes. Add the remaining ingredients and cook for a further 2–3 minutes.

★ Serve the prawn/shrimp balls hot or cold with the dipping sauce and with lime wedges to squeeze over them.

BRAZILIAN BLACK-EYED BEAN & SHRIMP FRITTERS

KNOWN AS *ACARAJÉ* IN BRAZIL, THESE FRITTERS ARE A POPULAR SNACK OF THE NORTHERN BAHIA REGION. THEY ARE TRADITIONALLY SOLD BY WHITE-ROBED WOMEN WEARING COLOURFUL HEADDRESSES.

200 g/1 cup dried black-eyed beans/peas, soaked overnight and drained

1 onion, chopped

2 chillies/chiles, red or green, chopped

½ teaspoon fish sauce

1 egg white, lightly beaten

1 teaspoon sea salt

125 g/4 oz. peeled prawns/shrimp, chopped

vegetable oil, for frying

salsa

1 red onion, finely chopped

1 tomato, skinned and chopped

1 garlic clove, finely chopped

2 tablespoons olive oil

1 tablespoon freshly squeezed lime juice

1 chilli/chile, green or red, finely chopped

1 tablespoon freshly chopped coriander/cilantro

sea salt and freshly ground black pepper

makes about 24

★ Put the black-eyed beans/peas in a saucepan, cover with 3 times their volume of water and bring to the boil. Simmer for 2 minutes, then take the pan off the heat and leave to soak in the water for 4 hours. Drain off the water and put the beans/peas into a food processor. Pulse briefly to break the skins, then add enough water to cover them and pulse again. Some of the beans/peas will break up, but that doesn't matter. Transfer the beans/peas and water to a large bowl and put in the sink. Rub the beans/peas vigorously with your fingers to loosen the skins, then put the pan under the cold tap/faucet, swishing the beans around so that the skins rise to the surface and can be skimmed off and discarded. Drain the beans/peas thoroughly when most of the skins have gone.

★ In a food processor, blend the beans/peas, onion, chilli/chile, fish sauce, egg white and salt with 125 ml/½ cup of water to make a paste. Add the chopped prawns/shrimp and mix well to incorporate them, then cover and leave this batter in the fridge for 1 hour.

★ Mix all of the salsa ingredients together in a bowl.

★ Heat the oil in a saucepan – it should be at least 5 cm/2 inches deep so that the fritters are covered. When the oil is hot, slip dessert-spoonfuls of the batter into the hot oil and fry in batches until golden brown on all sides, making sure they are fully cooked through. Drain on paper towels and serve hot with the salsa.

CRAB CAKE BALLS

300 g/10 oz. white crab meat

2 spring onions/scallions, finely chopped

a small handful of fresh flat-leaf parsley, finely chopped

1 red chilli/chile, deseeded and finely chopped

zest of 1 lemon and 1–2 teaspoons freshly squeezed juice

100 g/1⅓ cups fresh breadcrumbs

200 g/¾ cup mayonnaise

sea salt and freshly ground black pepper

1 teaspoon saffron fronds/threads

1 egg, beaten

sunflower oil, for frying

a handful of rocket/arugula leaves, to garnish

extra virgin olive oil, for drizzling

makes 12

THESE CRAB CAKES ARE GREAT AS INDIVIDUAL APPETIZERS, OR YOU COULD MAKE A LARGE SHARING PLATTER OF THEM WITH BOWLS OF THE MAYONNAISE TO DIP INTO. THE SAFFRON GIVES AN EARTHY FLAVOUR, WHICH IS LOVELY PAIRED WITH SWEET CRAB.

★ Squeeze any excess liquid out of the crab meat and add to a bowl together with the spring onions/scallions, most of the parsley, chilli/chile, the lemon zest, lemon juice, 50 g/⅔ cup of the fresh breadcrumbs and 5 tablespoons of the mayonnaise. Season with sea salt and black pepper and mix everything together until well combined. Divide the mixture into 12 equal portions using damp hands and form into slightly flattened balls. Refrigerate for 30 minutes.

★ Meanwhile, make the saffron mayonnaise. Put the saffron fronds/threads in a bowl and cover with 1 teaspoon of hot water. Give it a stir and leave to infuse for at least 5 minutes. Add to the remaining mayonnaise and stir to combine.

★ Dip the chilled crab cakes in the beaten egg and then roll in the remaining breadcrumbs until evenly covered. Set aside.

★ Pour 2.5 cm/1 inch of sunflower oil into a frying pan/skillet. Place over a medium heat until a piece of bread dropped into the oil browns in about 40 seconds. Carefully place the crab cakes in the oil and fry for 3 minutes on each side until crisp and golden. Remove with a slotted spoon and drain on paper towels.

★ Plate up the crab cakes with the rocket/arugula leaves twisted in and around them and the saffron mayonnaise dolloped on top. Drizzle over some extra virgin olive oil and scatter over the remaining chopped parsley. Serve immediately.

CHEDDAR CHEESE & TUNA FISH BALLS

4–5 tablespoons olive oil, for frying

cooked linguine, to serve

tuna fish balls

2 thick slices white bread, crusts removed

2 x 250-g/9-oz. cans tuna in olive oil, drained

1 egg

150 g/1¾ cups mature/sharp Cheddar cheese, grated

sea salt and freshly ground black pepper

tomato sauce

3 tablespoons olive oil

1 onion, finely chopped

2 garlic cloves, crushed

400-g/14-oz. can chopped tomatoes

2 teaspoons caster/granulated sugar

a small handful of fresh basil leaves, torn (or ½ teaspoon dried oregano)

serves 4

THESE TASTY LITTLE FISH BALLS ARE SO SIMPLE TO MAKE AND THE GREAT THING IS THAT EVERYTHING YOU NEED CAN PROBABLY BE FOUND IN YOUR KITCHEN CUPBOARD, MAKING THEM A BRILLIANT STANDBY IF YOU HAVE UNEXPECTED VISITORS FOR LUNCH.

★ To make the tuna fish balls, cut the crusts off the bread and whiz the bread in a food processor until you get crumbs. Transfer the breadcrumbs to a bowl with the tuna and stir until well mixed. Crack the egg into the bowl, then add the Cheddar cheese. Season with salt and black pepper.

★ Take a small amount of the tuna mixture in your hands and roll it around between damp palms to make a walnut-sized ball. Repeat with the rest of the mixture until there is none left. Set the fish balls aside.

★ To make the tomato sauce, heat the olive oil in a saucepan and fry the onion and garlic over a gentle heat for 4–5 minutes, until the onion has softened but not coloured. Add the canned tomatoes and sugar to the saucepan and season with a little salt and black pepper. Leave the sauce to bubble for about 10–15 minutes, until glossy and thick, then add the basil and leave the mixture to simmer gently for 5 minutes more.

★ Heat the olive oil in a frying pan/skillet and fry the fish balls for about 4–5 minutes, until hot and golden. Transfer them to a dish and pour the tomato sauce over the top. Serve with linguine.

SMOKED MACKEREL, POTATO & DILL BALLS

----

500 g/1 lb. 2 oz. potatoes, peeled and cut into chunks

1 tablespoon butter

350 g/12½ oz. smoked mackerel fillets, skinned

grated zest and juice of 1 lemon

15 g/½ cup fresh dill, finely chopped

1 teaspoon grain mustard

salt and freshly ground black pepper

2 tablespoons plain/all-purpose flour, for dusting

2–3 tablespoons vegetable oil, for frying

horseradish dipping sauce

150 ml/⅔ cup double/heavy cream

2 teaspoons white wine vinegar

1 teaspoon grain mustard

2 tablespoons grated horseradish

to serve

lemon wedges

crisp green salad

makes 12

THESE FISH BALLS HAVE A MOREISH COMBINATION OF FLAVOURS. THE SHARPNESS OF THE LEMON AND SLIGHTLY ANISEED FLAVOUR OF THE DILL CONTRAST BEAUTIFULLY WITH THE SMOKED MACKEREL. QUICK AND EASY TO PREPARE, THEY MAKE AN EXCELLENT LIGHT SUPPER OR EVEN BRUNCH DISH, TOPPED WITH A POACHED EGG OF COURSE.

★ Boil or steam the potatoes until tender. Drain and mash with the butter until smooth. Leave to cool completely.

★ Break the fish into small pieces and place in a bowl with the lemon zest and juice, dill, mustard and seasoning. Add the potato and mix until well combined. With lightly floured hands, form the mixture into 12 balls, then flatten each slightly to measure approximately 7 cm/3 inches x 1 cm/½ inch. Dust each with flour, shaking off the excess. Arrange on a plate or baking sheet lined with baking parchment. Cover loosely with clingfilm/plastic wrap and chill in the fridge for 30 minutes to firm up.

★ Heat the oil in a heavy-based frying pan/skillet over a medium heat. Fry the balls, a few at a time, for 6 minutes until a crust develops on the underside. Turn over carefully and cook for a further 4–6 minutes until evenly browned. Drain on paper towels. Keep the fish cakes warm until required.

★ For the horseradish dipping sauce, whip the cream until soft peaks form. Stir in the vinegar, mustard and horseradish and mix until well combined.

★ Serve the mackerel, potato and dill balls with the dip, lemon wedges and a crisp green salad.

SALT COD, POTATO & BUTTER BEAN FRITTERS

400 g/14 oz. salt cod

200 g/7 oz. floury potatoes, peeled and quartered

50 g/3 tablespoons canned butter/lima beans, drained and well rinsed

2 tablespoons whole milk

2 tablespoons olive oil

2 garlic cloves, crushed

2 tablespoons plain/all-purpose flour

¼ teaspoon baking powder

2 eggs, separated

2 spring onions/scallions, finely chopped

a small handful of fresh flat-leaf parsley leaves, finely chopped

light olive oil, for frying

lemon wedges, to serve

makes about 36

POTATOES MAKE THE PERFECT PARTNER TO THE FULL-FLAVOURED SALT COD IN THESE LIGHT AND CRISPY FRITTERS. THEY ARE THE TRADITIONAL INGREDIENTS, BUT THE ADDITION OF BUTTER/LIMA BEANS TO THE MIX MAKES THESE BALLS OF DELIGHT EXTRA SMOOTH AND CREAMY.

★ Soak the salt cod in cold water for 24 hours, changing the water every 6 hours.

★ Cook the potatoes in boiling water for 15 minutes, until tender. Add the beans and cook for 5 minutes. Drain well and put into a bowl. Mash with the milk and oil until chunky and well combined.

★ Drain the cod and cut into large chunks. Put into a saucepan and add sufficient water to fully submerge the cod. Bring to the boil and cook for 10–15 minutes, until the water surface is frothy and the fish is tender. Drain and leave to cool for a few minutes. When cool enough to handle, pick out any bones and flake the flesh with a fork.

★ Add the cod to the potatoes with the garlic, flour, baking powder, egg yolks, spring onions/scallions and parsley. Whisk the egg whites until peaking then fold into the potato mixture until combined.

★ Fill a heavy-based saucepan one-third full with oil and heat over a medium–high heat. The oil is ready when the surface is shimmering and a pinch of the fritter mixture sizzles on contact.

★ Drop heaped tablespoons of the fritter mixture into the hot oil, without overcrowding the pan, and cook for about 2 minutes, until golden and puffed. Transfer to a plate lined with paper towels and serve.

CHAPTER 6
VEGETARIAN

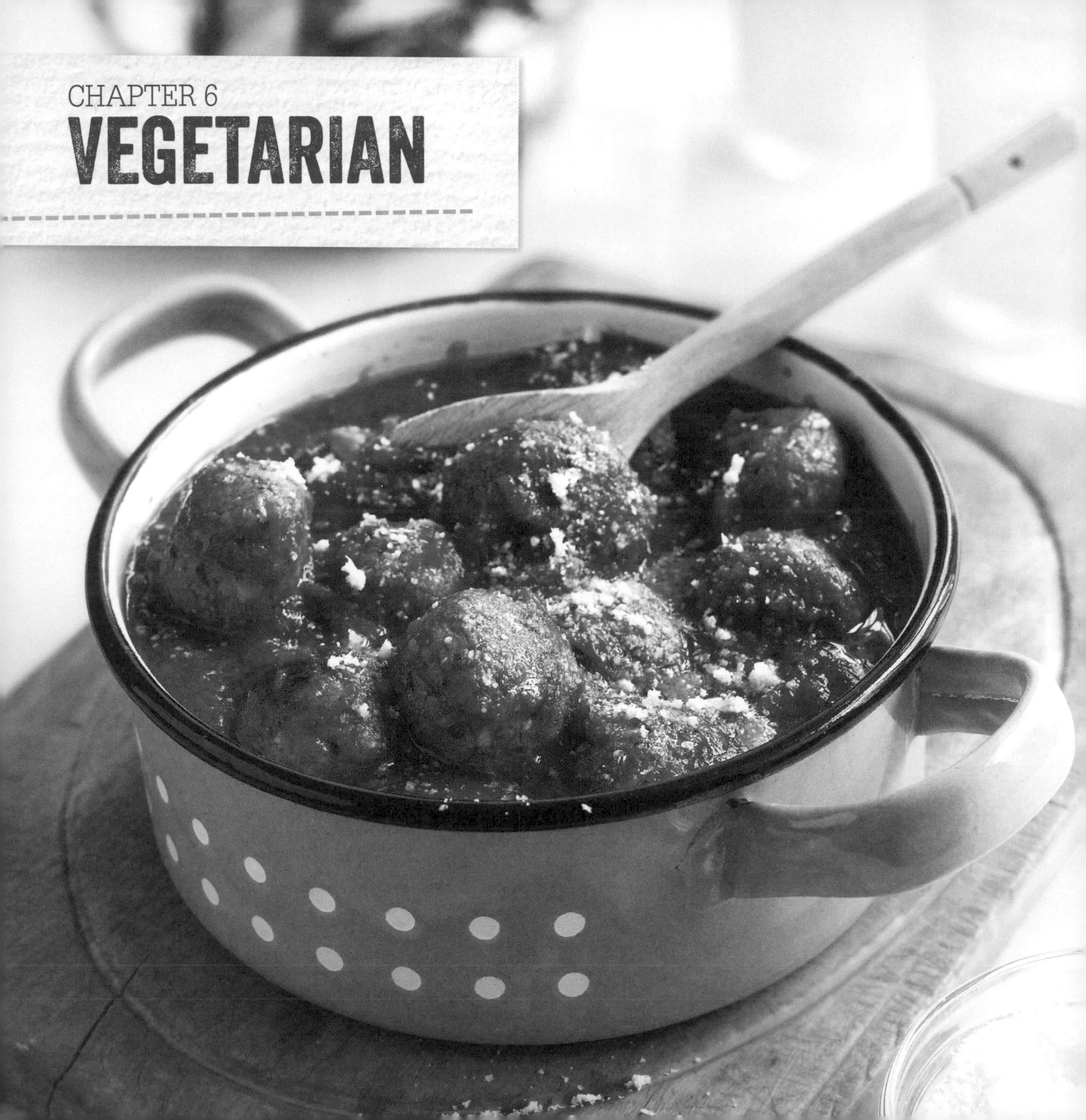

NUTTY MEATBALLS

250 g/2½ cups mixed nuts (walnuts, cashews, almonds and chestnuts)

100 g/generous 1½ cups wholemeal/whole-wheat breadcrumbs

2 medium onions, peeled and quartered

1 celery stick

1 small carrot

2–3 garlic cloves, peeled

leaves from a small bunch of fresh flat-leaf parsley

3–5 tablespoons olive oil

1 teaspoon dried thyme

2 teaspoons vegetable bouillon powder

1 egg, beaten

1–2 tablespoons whole milk

sea salt and freshly ground black pepper

to serve (optional)

1 quantity Tomato Sauce (see page 11)

wholewheat spaghetti or penne

finely grated Parmesan or Italian-style hard cheese

serves 4–6

THE BEAUTY LIES IN THE SIMPLICITY OF THIS NUT LOAF INSPIRED RECIPE. THERE ARE NOT TOO MANY FUSSY INGREDIENTS OR COMPLICATED PROCEDURES, JUST BLITZ UP THIS MIXTURE USING QUALITY PRODUCTS AND IT WILL TASTE FANTASTIC. TRY IT FOR YOURSELF AND SEE.

★ Preheat the oven to 180°C (350°F) Gas 4.

★ Process the nuts in a food processor until finely ground. Add to the breadcrumbs, season lightly and set aside.

★ Process the onions, celery, carrot, garlic cloves and parsley in the food processor until finely chopped.

★ Heat 3 tablespoons of the oil in a large frying pan/skillet. Add the onion mixture and thyme, season and cook for 5–7 minutes, until softened. Remove from the heat and let cool slightly.

★ Add the onion mixture to the nut mixture and stir well. Dissolve the bouillon powder in 125 ml/½ cup hot water and add to the onion mixture. Stir well. Add the egg and mix to combine. If the mixture is very dry, add the milk, or some water, 1 tablespoon at a time. The mixture needs to be soft or the finished dish will be dry, but not too soft.

★ Use your hands to shape the mixture into golf-ball-sized balls and arrange them on a baking sheet. Bake in the preheated oven for about 35 minutes, until browned. Serve in warmed tomato sauce with pasta and finely grated cheese.

SPICY BEAN BALLS

350 g/2 cups large, skinless, dried broad/fava beans, soaked in cold water for 24 hours

6 garlic cloves, crushed

1–2 teaspoons sea salt

2 teaspoons ground cumin

2 teaspoons ground coriander

1 scant teaspoon chilli powder

1 teaspoon baking powder

a bunch of fresh flat-leaf parsley, finely chopped

a bunch of fresh coriander/cilantro, finely chopped, plus some for garnishing

4 spring onions/scallions, finely chopped

400 g/1⅔ cups thick, creamy yogurt

sea salt and freshly ground black pepper

sunflower oil, for frying

to serve

1 teaspoon sumac

harissa paste

toasted pitta/pita bread

a handful of small green chilli/chile peppers, to serve

serves 4–6

GREAT TAKEAWAY FOOD AND A TASTY MEZZE DISH, THE MIDDLE EASTERN SPECIALITY FALAFEL CAN BE PREPARED WITH DRIED CHICKPEAS OR DRIED BROAD/FAVA BEANS, OR A COMBINATION OF THE TWO. TUCK A COUPLE OF WARM FRESHLY FRIED FALAFEL INTO THE HOLLOW POCKET OF A TOASTED PITTA/PITA BREAD WITH A SPRINKLING OF ROUGHLY CHOPPED FLAT-LEAF PARSLEY AND CHILLI/CHILE PEPPERS OF YOUR CHOICE; ADD A LITTLE CHILLI PASTE, SUCH AS HARISSA AND MAYBE A DOLLOP OF YOGURT, AND YOU HAVE THE MOST DELICIOUSLY HEALTHY MIDDLE EASTERN EQUIVALENT TO A FAST-FOOD BURGER. WHAT'S NOT TO LOVE?

★ Drain the broad/fava beans, put them into a food processor and blend to a smooth soft paste – this can take quite a long time. Add 4 of the crushed garlic cloves, salt, cumin, coriander, chilli powder and baking powder and continue to blend the paste. Add most of the parsley, the coriander/cilantro and spring onions/scallions and blend the mixture briefly. Leave the mixture to rest for 1–2 hours.

★ Meanwhile, beat the yogurt in a bowl with the remaining garlic cloves. Season well to taste and put aside.

★ Mould the broad/fava bean mixture into small, tight balls and place them on a plate. Heat up enough oil for deep-frying in a pan and fry the broad/fava bean balls in batches, until golden brown. Drain them on paper towels.

★ Tip the falafel onto a serving dish and garnish with the reserved coriander/cilantro. Serve them with the yogurt mixture, sprinkled with sumac, along with harissa paste, toasted pitta/pita bread and chilli/chile peppers.

200 g/7 oz. mashed potato, cooled

200 g/7 oz. paneer cheese, grated

½ teaspoon each chilli powder and ground cardamom

2 tablespoons cornflour/cornstarch

salt and freshly ground black pepper

filling

25 g/scant ¼ cup cashew nuts, chopped

1 tablespoon raisins, chopped

sauce

1 tablespoon vegetable oil

1 tablespoon butter

2 onions, chopped

2 garlic cloves, crushed

2.5-cm/1-inch piece fresh ginger, peeled and grated

2 teaspoons poppy seeds

25 g/scant ¼ cup cashew nuts, finely ground

400-g/14-oz. can chopped tomatoes

1 teaspoon chilli powder

½ teaspoon each garam masala, ground coriander, ground cumin and caster/granulated sugar

to serve

125 ml/scant ½ cup single/light cream

50 g/½ cup flaked/slivered almonds

freshly chopped coriander/cilantro

naan breads, warmed

a deep-fat fryer

makes 8

MALAI KOFTA WITH FRUIT & NUT FILLING

MALAI KOFTAS ARE A TRADITIONAL RECIPE FROM NORTHERN INDIA MADE FROM SPICED PANEER CHEESE AND POTATOES WITH A SWEET FRUIT AND NUT FILLING. THEY ARE OFTEN SERVED AT DIWALI CELEBRATIONS.

★ In a large bowl, add the potato, cheese, chilli powder, cardamom, cornflour/cornstarch, salt and pepper. Mix together well, then use your hands to combine together to give a smooth, dough-like consistency.

★ For the filling, mix together the cashew nuts and raisins. Shape the potato into 8 equal golf-ball-sized balls. Take one ball and mould into a cup shape with your fingers. Place a little of the filling mixture into the centre then pinch the potato back around the filling to seal it, shaping the ball back into a round. Repeat with the remaining potato and filling. Arrange the balls on a plate. Cover with clingfilm/plastic wrap and chill for 1 hour.

★ For the sauce, heat the oil and butter in a large saucepan over a medium heat. Add the onions, garlic, ginger and poppy seeds, reduce the heat to low and cover the pan. Cook the onions very slowly, stirring occasionally for about 30 minutes until very soft. Stir in the remaining ingredients. Cool slightly then transfer to a food processor and purée. Return the sauce to the pan, bring to the boil stirring well, then reduce the heat to simmer and cook for 10–15 minutes, stirring frequently, adding water if the consistency is too thick. Set aside whilst cooking the koftas.

★ Preheat the oil in the deep-fat fryer to 180°C (350°F). Fry the koftas a few at a time for a few minutes until golden brown. Drain on paper towels. Add them to the sauce and heat through well. Drizzle with cream, sprinkle with the almonds and coriander/cilantro and serve with naan bread.

NAKED SPINACH & RICOTTA 'RAVIOLI'

1 kg/2 lbs. 3 oz. fresh spinach, well washed and roughly chopped

250 g/generous 1 cup ricotta cheese

5 egg yolks

125 g/2 cups Parmesan or Italian-style hard cheese, finely grated, plus extra to serve

125 g/1 cup plain/all-purpose flour

1 tablespoon butter

12 fresh sage leaves

250 ml/generous 1 cup single/light cream

sea salt and freshly ground black pepper

a baking sheet, lined with baking parchment

serves 3–4

MISSING THE PASTA WRAPPING THAT USUALLY ENCLOSES THE FILLING (HENCE 'NAKED'), THESE LIGHT AND CLASSY 'RAVIOLI' ARE A GREAT OPTION FOR ANYONE ON A BUDGET, AS THEY REQUIRE JUST A FEW SIMPLE INGREDIENTS AND TAKE NO TIME AT ALL TO MAKE.

★ Bring a large pan of water to the boil. Add the spinach and cook for 5 minutes, until wilted and tender. Rinse with cold water and drain well.

★ Tip the cooked spinach into the centre of a clean kitchen cloth. (This process will stain it, so use an old, threadbare one, rather than your best.) Roll the kitchen cloth up to form a log and twist the ends away from each other to squeeze out as much liquid as possible. Put the spinach on a chopping board and chop finely. Transfer to a large bowl. Add the ricotta, egg yolks and half of the Parmesan or Italian-style hard cheese and season to taste with salt and pepper. Mix well to thoroughly combine.

★ Put the flour on a large plate. Using damp hands, roll the spinach mixture into 12 walnut-sized balls. Lightly roll each ball in the flour and put them on the prepared baking sheet.

★ Put the butter and sage in a small saucepan and set over a medium heat. Cook until the sage leaves just sizzle. Add the cream and the remaining Italian-style hard cheese and cook for about 10 minutes, until thickened, stirring to prevent the cream from catching on the bottom of the pan.

★ Bring a large saucepan of lightly salted water to the boil. Carefully drop the balls into the boiling water and cook for just 1 minute, until they rise to the surface. Drain well and arrange 4 balls in each serving dish. Spoon over the warm sage cream, sprinkle with the extra Italian-style hard cheese and grind over plenty of black pepper. Serve immediately.

SPANISH CHEESE BALLS

2 tablespoons plain/all-purpose flour

2 tablespoons whole milk

½ teaspoon sweet smoked Spanish paprika

1 egg

1 garlic clove, crushed

150 g/5½ oz. Manchego cheese, finely grated

150 g/5½ oz. goats' cheese, preferably Spanish

2 egg whites

1 teaspoon freshly chopped thyme leaves

sea salt and freshly ground white pepper

oil, for frying

a deep-fat fryer

serves 4

MANCHEGO CHEESE IS POPULAR ALL OVER SPAIN. IT IS TO THE SPANISH WHAT PARMESAN IS TO THE ITALIANS. THE MIX OF MANCHEGO SHEEPS' CHEESE AND SPANISH GOATS' CHEESE BALANCES EACH OTHER PERFECTLY. A REAL TREAT FOR YOUR DINNER GUESTS.

★ Put the flour and milk in a bowl and stir until smooth. Add the paprika, salt and a generous grinding of pepper and the whole egg. Add the garlic and both cheeses and mix well.

★ Put the egg whites in a bowl and whisk until stiff. Fold one-third into the flour mixture and mix well, then fold in the remaining egg whites making sure not to lose all the air. Sprinkle with the thyme leaves.

★ Fill a deep-fat fryer with oil to the manufacturer's recommended level and heat the oil to 195°C (380°F). Drop heaped spoonfuls of the cheese mixture into the hot oil. Cook for 3 minutes or until the balls are golden brown. Drain on paper towels and serve immediately with cocktail sticks/toothpicks.

LEMON & MUSHROOM RISOTTO BALLS

2 tablespoons butter or olive oil

1 onion, finely chopped

150 g/2½ cups finely chopped chestnut mushrooms

15 g/½ oz. dried porcini mushrooms, soaked in hot water until soft, then finely chopped (reserve the liquid)

1 garlic clove, crushed

grated zest of 1 lemon and juice from ½ a lemon

100 g/½ cup risotto rice

150 ml/⅔ cup dry white wine

300 ml/1¼ cups vegetable stock

a small bunch of fresh flat-leaf parsley

50 g/⅔ cup grated Parmesan or Italian-style hard cheese

5-mm/¼-inch cubes red (bell) pepper

500 ml/about 2 cups vegetable oil, for frying

salt and black pepper

mayonnaise, to serve (optional)

breadcrumb coating

50 g/⅓ cup plus 1 tablespoon plain/all-purpose flour, seasoned

1 egg, lightly beaten

100 g/1¼ cups dried breadcrumbs

a deep-fat fryer

makes 16

ARANCINI (SICILIAN STUFFED RICE BALLS) ARE A GREAT WAY TO SERVE RISOTTO. THEY MAKE A VERY SATISFYING BITE-SIZED NIBBLE.

★ Melt the butter in a heavy-based saucepan set over a low heat. Add the onion and cook gently for about 10 minutes, then add the mushrooms and cook until softened. Add the garlic and cook for another minute. Turn up the heat to medium and add the lemon zest and rice. Stir well and until the rice becomes opaque. Add the white wine, if using, and stir until all the liquid has been absorbed. Repeat this process with about 200 ml/¾ cup of the stock. Add any leftover mushroom liquid. Stir well until the liquid has been absorbed, then keep adding stock and stirring until the rice is cooked (about 20 minutes) – the rice will have softened but still have a slight bite. Make sure the liquid is well evaporated – the consistency should be thicker than a risotto. Stir the Parmesan or Italian-style hard cheese and parsley through.

★ Spread the rice on a large plate or tray to cool it quickly, then form it into 16 bite-sized balls. To fill the balls, put each one in the palm of your hand and push down into the centre with your thumb, and put a few red (bell) pepper cubes in, then cover with the rice and roll back into a ball.

★ For the breadcrumb coating, put the flour, lightly beaten egg and breadcrumbs in three separate bowls. Roll each ball in the flour and tap off any excess. Then roll in egg and then in the breadcrumbs. Put in the fridge.

★ Fill a deep-fat fryer with vegetable oil or pour oil to a depth of about 5 cm/2 inches into a deep saucepan. Heat until a cube of bread sizzles and browns in about 5 seconds. Cook in batches until golden brown (1–2 minutes).

ARANCINI WITH PECORINO, PORCINI & MOZZARELLA

15 g/½ oz. dried porcini mushrooms

1 tablespoon olive oil

2 tablespoons unsalted butter

2 shallots, finely chopped

1 fat garlic clove, crushed

250 g/1¼ cups risotto rice

760–860 ml/3–3½ cups vegetable stock

40 g/⅓ cup grated pecorino cheese

1 tablespoon freshly chopped flat-leaf parsley or oregano

125 g/4 oz. mozzarella cheese, diced

100 g/¾ cup plain/all-purpose flour

2 eggs, lightly beaten

200 g/3 cups fresh, fine breadcrumbs

about 1 litre/4 cups sunflower oil, for frying

sea salt and freshly ground black pepper

a deep-fat fryer

makes 15–18

YOU CAN USE LEFTOVER RISOTTO FOR THESE MUSHROOM & MOZZARELLA RICE BALLS IF YOU HAPPEN TO HAVE ANY, BUT AS THEY ARE SO DELICIOUS IT'S WORTH MAKING THE RISOTTO SPECIALLY FOR THEM.

★ Soak the porcini in a small bowl of boiling water for about 15 minutes, or until soft. Drain well on paper towels and finely chop.

★ Heat the olive oil and butter in a medium saucepan and add the shallots, garlic and chopped porcini. Cook over low–medium heat until soft but not coloured. Add the rice to the pan and stir to coat well in the buttery mixture. Gradually add the vegetable stock – add it one ladleful at a time, and as the stock is absorbed by the rice, add another ladleful, stirring as you do so. Continue cooking in this way until the rice is al dente and the stock is used up. Remove the pan from the heat, add the pecorino and herbs and season well with salt and black pepper. Tip the risotto into a bowl and let cool completely.

★ Once the rice is cold, divide it into walnut-sized pieces and roll into balls. Taking one ball at a time, flatten it into a disc in the palm of your hand, press some diced mozzarella in the middle and wrap the rice around it to completely encase the cheese. Shape into a neat ball. Repeat with the remaining risotto.

★ Tip the flour, beaten eggs and breadcrumbs into separate shallow bowls. Roll the rice balls first in the flour, then coat well in the eggs and finally, roll them in the breadcrumbs to completely coat.

★ Fill a deep-fat fryer with sunflower oil or pour oil to a depth of about 5 cm/ 2 inches into a deep saucepan. Heat until a cube of bread sizzles and browns in about 5 seconds. Cook the arancini, in batches, in the hot oil for 3–4 minutes or until crisp, hot and golden brown. Drain on paper towels.

OLIVE *SUPPLÌ*

17 cured black olives, stoned/pitted

40 g/⅓ cup plain/all-purpose flour

2 eggs, beaten

140 g/generous 2 cups fresh breadcrumbs

vegetable oil, for frying

saffron salt, to sprinkle

risotto

20 g/scant 1 cup dried porcini mushrooms

250 ml/1 cup white wine

500 ml/2 cups vegetable stock

2 tablespoons olive oil

1 garlic clove, finely chopped

2 tablespoons thyme leaves

1 tablespoon freshly chopped rosemary

200 g risotto rice

60 g/1 cup Parmesan or Italian-style hard cheese, grated

sea salt and cracked black pepper

a deep-fat fryer

makes 17

TRADITIONAL *SUPPLÌ* HAVE MOZZARELLA INSIDE AND ARE KNOWN IN ROME AS *SUPPLÌ AL TELEFONO*, BECAUSE WHEN YOU BITE INTO THEM THE MOZZARELLA PULLS INTO STRANDS AND LOOKS LIKE A TELEPHONE WIRE. HIDING A SALTY CURED BLACK OLIVE IN THE CENTRE OF THESE CRISPY BALLS INSTEAD MAKES FOR A DELICIOUS SURPRISE.

★ For the risotto, soak the mushrooms in the wine for 30 minutes. Drain, reserving the liquid, and chop roughly. Pour the reserved liquid into a small saucepan with the vegetable stock. Bring to the boil and reduce to a simmer. Put the olive oil, garlic, thyme, rosemary and mushrooms in a medium saucepan and cook over medium–high heat for a few seconds, coating with the olive oil. Add the rice and stir for 2–3 minutes until well coated and translucent. Start adding the stock a ladleful at a time, stirring continuously until the liquid has been absorbed. Continue until you have used all the liquid, about 20 minutes. Stir in the cheese and season with salt and black pepper. Pour onto a large plate and spread out to cool.

★ To make the supplì, take tablespoons of cooled risotto and form 17 balls. With your index finger, make a dent in each risotto ball and place an olive in the centre. Roll the risotto ball in your hand to reshape and cover the olive.

★ Dust the supplì balls with flour, dip into the beaten egg and then toss in the breadcrumbs until well coated. At this stage they can be left to rest in the fridge for up to 6 hours until you are ready to cook.

★ Heat the oil in a heavy-bottomed pan until the oil reaches 180°C (350°F) on a deep-frying thermometer. Alternatively, test the oil by dropping in a cube of bread. It should turn golden brown in about 20 seconds. Fry the supplì in batches until crispy and golden brown, about 2 minutes. Drain on paper towels. Sprinkle generously with saffron salt and serve.

sea salt and freshly ground black pepper

falafel

120 g/1 cup pumpkin seeds

60 g/½ cup each sunflower seeds and walnuts

50 g/½ cup each fresh basil and fresh flat-leaf parsley

6 sundried tomatoes, soaked for about 1 hour in warm water

½ teaspoon dried oregano

½ teaspoon dried mixed Mediterranean herbs, e.g. thyme, savory, marjoram, rosemary, fennel

2 garlic cloves, crushed

1–2 tablespoons olive oil

1 tablespoon freshly squeezed lemon juice, or to taste

tahini sauce

4 tablespoons tahini

60 ml/¼ cup warm water

1 teaspoon umeboshi vinegar

1 garlic clove, crushed

1 tablespoon snipped chives

freshly squeezed lemon juice, to taste

tamari soy sauce, to taste

to serve

3–4 cos/Romaine lettuce leaves

10–12 slices of tomato

a small handful of grated courgette/zucchini

a small handful of grated carrot

2 tablespoons sliced spring onions/scallions

makes 10–12

'RAW' FALAFEL

SOME PEOPLE LOVE FALAFEL BUT DON'T LIKE TO EAT DEEP-FRIED FOODS, OR HAVE DIFFICULTY DIGESTING THE SOAKED CHICKPEAS. HERE'S A RAW AND CHICKPEA-FREE VERSION THAT IS SURPRISINGLY EASY TO MAKE. THEY WILL FILL YOU UP FOR MANY HOURS! THE FRESH TAHINI SAUCE FLAVOURED WITH LEMON, GARLIC AND CHIVES COMPLEMENTS THE FLAVOURS PERFECTLY.

★ For the falafel, put the seeds in a coffee grinder and grind to fine flour. Very finely chop the walnuts, basil, parsley and drained sun-dried tomatoes. Combine all the ingredients with salt and pepper to taste, and mix well with your hands or a silicone spatula. Wrap in clingfilm/plastic wrap and refrigerate for 30 minutes. Or, if in a hurry, make them right away. Pull off portions of the mixture about the size of small walnuts and roll into balls.

★ For the tahini sauce, mix all the ingredients well and allow to stand for 20 minutes before serving. It keeps well in the fridge, so make double or triple, ready for the next batch of falafels.

★ To serve, put 2–3 falafels on a lettuce leaf with some tomato, courgette/zucchini and carrot and spring onions/scallions. Top with a drizzle of tahini sauce. Eat with a knife and fork or roll up like a wrap and eat with your fingers.

WINTER VEGETABLE STEW WITH HERBED DUMPLINGS

- 2 tablespoons olive oil
- 2 tablespoons butter
- 3 shallots, quartered
- 2 white potatoes, cut into chunks
- 1 parsnip, cut into chunks
- 250 g/9 oz. baby chantenay carrots, left whole
- 250 g/4 cups button mushrooms
- 1 leek, sliced into rings
- 2 garlic cloves, crushed
- 4 sprigs fresh thyme
- 1 teaspoon Dijon mustard
- 2 tablespoons plain/all-purpose flour
- 1 tablespoon balsamic vinegar
- 240 ml/1 cup white wine
- 400-g/14-oz. can butter/lima beans
- 250 g/9 oz. fresh raw beetroot/beets, peeled and cut into chunks
- 300 ml/1¼ cups vegetable stock
- salt and freshly ground black pepper

herbed dumplings

- 250 g/2 cups minus 1½ tablespoons plain/all-purpose flour
- 2 teaspoons baking powder
- 125 g/1 stick plus 1 tablespoon salted butter, chilled
- a handful of fresh herbs
- pinch of mustard powder (optional)
- sea salt and freshly ground black pepper

serves 4

THIS VERSATILE STEW WITH HERBY DUMPLING BALLS IS PACKED WITH ROOT VEGETABLES, MAKING IT BOTH HEARTY AND HEALTHY.

★ Preheat the oven to 180°C (350°F) Gas 4. Put the oil and butter in a flameproof casserole dish set over a medium heat. Add the shallots and cook for 2 minutes. Add the other vegetables and cook for 5 minutes, stirring occasionally, until the vegetables start to turn golden. Reduce the heat slightly and add the garlic and thyme. Season generously, then stir in the mustard. Add the flour and stir until the vegetables are well coated and the flour has disappeared. Add the vinegar and wine and cook for 2 minutes. Add the beans and beetroot/beets, stir gently, then add the vegetable stock. Bring the mixture to the boil for 2 minutes. Cover with the lid and bake for 40–50 minutes.

★ Meanwhile, prepare the dumplings. Sift the flour and baking powder into a bowl. Chop the cold butter into small pieces, then rub it into the flour as if you were making pastry dough. When the mixture looks like breadcrumbs and there are no lumps of butter, stir in the chopped herbs, mustard powder, if using, and season. Add a couple of tablespoons of water, or enough to bring the mixture together to form a stiff dough. Divide the dough into walnut-sized balls. Cover with clingfilm/plastic wrap and chill in the fridge until the stew is cooked.

★ When the stew is ready, partly submerge the dumplings in it. Cover with a lid and return to the oven. Cook for 20 minutes until the dumplings have puffed up and are golden on the top.

RICOTTA & SPINACH BALLS WITH CHERRY TOMATO SAUCE

INSPIRED BY ITALIAN CUISINE, THIS RECIPE USES RICOTTA, TOGETHER WITH SPINACH, TO MAKE DELICATE LITTLE BALLS OF GOODNESS.

400 g/14 oz. fresh spinach, rinsed well

250 g/1 cup ricotta, placed in a kitchen cloth in a sieve/strainer over a bowl

2 eggs

100 g/¾ cup fine semolina, plus extra for coating

50 g/⅔ cup grated Parmesan or Italian-style hard cheese, plus extra for serving

salt and freshly ground black pepper

freshly grated nutmeg

butter, for greasing

cherry tomato sauce

2 tablespoons olive oil

2 garlic cloves, chopped

a splash of dry white wine (optional)

2 x 400-g/14-oz. cans peeled cherry tomatoes

2 pinches dried chilli/hot red pepper flakes or 1 peperoncino, crumbled

sprinkle of freshly grated lemon zest

generous handful of fresh basil leaves, reserving a few

serves 4

★ Put the spinach in a large saucepan and cook, covered, over a medium heat until it has just wilted. Strain and press out any excess moisture. Set aside to cool, then chop finely, again squeezing out any excess moisture.

★ For the sauce, heat the oil in a heavy-based frying pan/skillet. Add the garlic and fry, stirring, until golden brown. Add the white wine and cook, stirring, until it has largely evaporated. Add the tomatoes, chilli/hot red pepper flakes and zest. Roughly tear the basil and mix in. Season. Cook for 5–10 minutes, stirring now and then until the sauce has thickened.

★ Put the ricotta in a large bowl and break it up with a fork. Mix in the spinach thoroughly. Add the eggs, semolina and Parmesan or Italian-style hard cheese and mix well. Season with salt, pepper and nutmeg and mix again. Sprinkle semolina to lightly cover a large plate. Take a teaspoon of the ricotta mixture and, using a second teaspoon, shape it into a little nugget. Still using teaspoons, place this ricotta dumpling on the semolina and roll, lightly coating it. Repeat.

★ Preheat the oven to 190°C (350°F) Gas 5, and gently reheat the cherry tomato sauce. Put a buttered heatproof serving dish in the oven to warm. Line a plate with paper towels. Bring a large saucepan of salted water to the boil. Add the dumplings to the water in batches. Cook over a medium heat until they float to the surface, around 2–3 minutes. Remove using a slotted spoon, drain on the plate, then transfer to the serving dish in the oven to keep warm. Tear the remaining basil and stir into the sauce. Serve the dumplings with the sauce and extra Italian-style hard cheese.

POPCORN TOFU BALLS

6 tablespoons light soy sauce

2 teaspoons Chinese five-spice powder

400 g/14 oz. firm tofu, cut into bite-sized pieces

150 g/1 cups cornflour/cornstarch

100 ml/⅓ cup soya/soy cream

150 g/2¾ cups panko breadcrumbs

1 teaspoon hot smoked paprika

vegetable oil, for deep-frying

steamed jasmine rice or sticky rice (optional), to serve

plum sauce

12 plums, stoned/pitted and roughly chopped

4–6 tablespoons soft brown sugar

8 tablespoons rice vinegar, or to taste

1 tablespoon tomato purée/paste, or to taste

½ teaspoon salt

serves 4–6

THIS IS A FUSION-STYLE DISH THAT WORKS VERY WELL AS A SNACK OR APPETIZER. THERE ARE QUITE A LOT OF PROCESSES INVOLVED, BUT YOU CAN SAVE TIME BY USING A READY-MADE PLUM SAUCE, IF YOU LIKE. YOU CAN ALSO SERVE THESE AS A MAIN COURSE ALONG WITH STEAMED JASMINE OR STICKY RICE.

★ To make the sauce, put the plums in a pan over medium heat and add 2 tablespoons water and the sugar. Bring to the boil, then simmer for 15 minutes or until the fruit is completely softened. Add the remaining sauce ingredients and bring to a simmer again, adding a little water if necessary so that the sauce is not too thick. Using a food processor or blender, blend the sauce until smooth. Check the seasoning and adjust the sugar, salt or vinegar to taste. The balance of sweet-and-sour flavours means one should not overpower the other.

★ Mix the soy sauce and five-spice powder in a small bowl, then drizzle this marinade over the tofu pieces. Put the cornflour/cornstarch in one bowl, the soya/soy cream in another bowl and the panko breadcrumbs in a third bowl. Add the paprika to the panko breadcrumbs and mix well.

★ Heat 600 ml/2½ cups vegetable oil in a wok over medium–high heat. Put a sheet of greaseproof paper on the work surface. Dip each piece of tofu in the cornflour/cornstarch, then in the soya/soy cream and then in the breadcrumbs, shaping it a little to form a ball. Lay each coated ball on the greaseproof paper as you go.

★ Fry the tofu balls in batches, until golden brown and crispy. Lift out using a slotted spoon and drain on paper towels. You can keep the tofu balls warm in a low oven at 140°C (275°F) Gas 1, if you like, or reheat them later at 170°C (350°F) Gas 4 for 10–15 minutes. Serve with the plum sauce.

TOMATO *KEFTEDES*

THERE ARE PLENTY OF FLAVOURS AND TEXTURES AT PLAY IN THESE
GORGEOUS GREEK TOMATO FRITTERS. THEY ARE SIMPLY ONIONS AND
A MIXTURE OF GREEN HERBS BOUND TOGETHER WITH PINCHED TOMATO
FLESH AND FLOUR, THEN FRIED UNTIL GOLDEN AND CRISP.

400 g/14 oz. ripe cherry tomatoes

½ red onion, very finely chopped

a large handful of fresh basil, chopped

a large handful of fresh mint, chopped

1 teaspoon dried oregano

a large handful of fresh flat-leaf parsley, chopped

100 g/¾ cup self-raising/self-rising flour

250 ml/1½ cups olive oil

750 ml/3 cups sunflower or canola oil

tzatziki (see page 129), to serve

makes 16

★ For the tomato keftedes, put the tomatoes in a large bowl and pinch them so that the juices spurt out (be careful to pinch them facing downwards, otherwise you'll end up with pulp in your eye). Keep pinching and tearing at the flesh until you're left with a pile of seeds, juices and pulp. Add the onion, basil, mint, oregano, parsley and salt and pepper to the pulp. You can use a potato masher at this point to make sure everything is well incorporated.

★ Add half the flour and stir. Add the second half slowly. You want a thick and sticky paste the texture of a thick batter.

★ Heat the oils in a deep, heavy-based pan until small bubbles form on the surface. Make sure the oil is at least 5 cm/2 inches deep. Use a greased tablespoon to drop in the batter. After 30 seconds, rotate the fritter so it doesn't stick to the bottom. Fry for another 30 seconds or until the outside is crispy and deep red. Drain well on paper towels. Fry no more than 3 at a time.

★ Season the fritters with salt and serve hot with tzatziki.

YELLOW BEAN BALLS

PEOPLE HAVE LARGELY FORGOTTEN THAT THIS SO-CALLED
TRADITIONAL THAI DISH ORIGINATED IN INDIA. HOWEVER, IT HAS
BEEN ADAPTED TO SUIT THE THAI TASTE BY ADDING MORE FRESH
CHILLIES/CHILES. IT IS A BEAUTIFUL AND ELEGANT DISH OF MANY
FASCINATING FLAVOURS INCLUDING PLENTY OF KAFFIR LIME LEAVES.

250 g/1½ cups dried split mung
beans, soaked in water for 30
minutes and drained

1 tablespoon plain/all-purpose
flour

1 teaspoon red curry paste

2 tablespoons light soy sauce

2 teaspoons sugar

5 kaffir lime leaves, rolled into a
cylinder and finely sliced into
slivers

peanut or sunflower oil, for deep-
frying

thick sweet sauce

4 tablespoons caster/granulated
sugar

6 tablespoons rice vinegar

½ teaspoon salt

a deep-fat fryer (optional)

serves 4

★ To make the sauce, put the sugar, vinegar and salt in a small saucepan
or wok and heat gently until the sugar dissolves. Let cool before serving
with the bean balls.

★ To make the balls, pound the drained mung beans with a pestle and
mortar or use a blender to form a coarse paste. Stirring well after each
addition, add the flour, curry paste, soy sauce, sugar and kaffir lime
leaves. Pluck a small piece of the paste and form into a ball the size
of a walnut. Do not mould too tightly.

★ Fill a wok or deep-fryer one-third full with the oil or to the
manufacturer's recommended level. Heat until a scrap of noodle puffs
up immediately.

★ Working in batches if necessary, add the balls and fry until golden
brown. Remove with a slotted spoon, drain on paper towels and serve
with the thick sweet sauce.

- 120 g/1 cup cashew nuts
- 2 bottle/doodhi gourds, peeled and grated
- 375 g/3 cups chickpea/gram flour
- 2 large red chillies/chiles
- 1 teaspoon each ginger paste and garlic paste
- a large handful of fresh coriander/cilantro
- 1 teaspoon chaat masala
- 1 teaspoon salt, or to taste
- vegetable oil, for shallow-frying

masala sauce

- 2 aubergines/eggplants, roughly chopped
- 1 teaspoon salt, or to taste
- 2 tablespoons vegetable oil, plus extra to grease
- 2 onions, thinly sliced
- 1 tablespoon each ginger paste and garlic paste
- ½ teaspoon ground turmeric
- 1 teaspoon ground cumin
- 2 teaspoons ground coriander
- 1 teaspoon Kashmiri chilli powder, or ½ teaspoon chilli powder and ½ teaspoon paprika
- 4 small green chillies/chiles, finely chopped
- 2 x 400-g/14-oz. cans chopped tomatoes
- 1 teaspoon garam masala
- 1 heaped tablespoon dried methi/fenugreek leaves, or ½ bunch of fresh leaves, roughly chopped

a baking sheet, greased

serves 4–6

DOODHI BOTTLE GOURD KOFTA MASALA

DOODHI IS A TYPE OF INDIAN GOURD, WHICH IS SOLD IN MANY INDIAN GROCERS. THIS RECIPE USES THE BOTTLE GOURD, WHICH LOOKS LIKE A LIGHT-GREEN ELONGATED SQUASH.

★ Toast the cashew nuts in a dry pan/skillet over medium heat for 1–2 minutes, stirring occasionally, until golden. Put the grated gourds in a colander and drain the excess liquid, squeezing the grated flesh to remove as much water as possible. Put the flour in a bowl and add the chillies/chiles, cashews, ginger and garlic pastes, fresh coriander/cilantro, chaat masala and salt. Add 240–360 ml/1–1½ cups water to form a thick paste. Taste the paste and add more salt if necessary.

★ Half-fill a frying pan/skillet with oil and place over a medium heat. Wet your hands and form the mixture into 16–18 loose balls each about the size of a golf ball. Gently drop the koftas into the oil and fry in batches until golden brown and cooked through. Drain on paper towels.

★ Preheat the oven to 220°C (425°F) Gas 7.

★ For the sauce, put the aubergines/eggplants on the prepared baking sheet and sprinkle with salt. Roast for 20–30 minutes until browned. Heat the oil in a large pan over a medium heat and cook the onions for 5 minutes or until softened. Add the ginger, garlic, spices and chillies/chiles, then fry for 3 minutes more. Add the tomatoes and garam masala. Bring to the boil, then simmer gently for 10–15 minutes until thickened. Add the aubergines/eggplants and simmer for 10 minutes or until the mixture is thick. Using a hand-held blender, blend to smooth. Add the methi/fenugreek and stir. Season to taste with salt. Add the koftas and simmer gently, being careful not to break the koftas. Serve.

SWEET POTATO, KALE & QUINOA BALLS

THESE BALLS ARE DELICIOUS AND CONTAIN INGREDIENTS PACKED WITH PLENTY OF GOODNESS –
PROTEIN-RICH QUINOA, VITAMIN C-PACKED SWEET POTATO AND OF COURSE, KALE – THE
ULTIMATE SUPERFOOD. THEY ARE EQUALLY NICE SERVED WARM AS A LIGHT AND SUMMERY
MAIN MEAL WITH A SIMPLE SALAD, OR EATEN COLD IN A PACKED LUNCH. HERE THEY ARE FRIED
IN COCONUT OIL TO GIVE A CRISPY FINISH, BUT YOU CAN OVEN BAKE INSTEAD IF YOU PREFER.

2 medium sweet potatoes, peeled
and cut into cubes

100 g/½ cup plus 1½ tablespoons
uncooked quinoa

25 g/1 oz. kale, stalks and veins
removed, finely shredded

1 carrot, grated

1 small onion, grated

2 eggs

50 g/1¾ oz. milled organic
linseeds/flaxseeds

3 teaspoons tapioca flour

1 teaspoon paprika

sea salt and freshly ground black
pepper

2–3 tablespoons coconut oil,
for frying

green leaves, radicchio leaves
and lemon wedges, to serve

a selection of dips, to serve

makes 12

★ Steam or boil the sweet potato for 15–20 minutes until tender. Transfer
to a large bowl and mash thoroughly. Allow to cool completely.

★ Bring 300 ml/1¼ cups water to the boil in a large saucepan. Rinse the
quinoa several times and add to the water. Reduce the heat to simmer and
cook, covered, for 20 minutes until most of the water has been absorbed
and the quinoa is fully cooked but still al dente. Drain and leave to stand
for 10 minutes then fluff up the grains with a fork.

★ Spoon the quinoa into a large bowl. Add the kale, carrot, onion, eggs,
linseeds/flaxseeds, tapioca flour, paprika, salt and pepper and mix together
until thoroughly combined. With wet hands, shape the mixture into 12 balls,
then flatten each slightly. Arrange on a plate or baking sheet lined with
baking parchment.

★ Heat the oil in a heavy-based frying pan/skillet until very hot. Add the
balls a few at a time and cook for 3–4 minutes, turning them once until
golden brown. Drain on paper towels.

★ Serve with green leaves and radicchio leaves, lemon wedges for squeezing
and a selection of dips (see pages 128–129).

500 ml/2¼ cups dried chickpeas

1 medium onion, quartered

2 teaspoons salt

pinch of freshly ground black pepper

2–3 garlic cloves

2–3 slices stale bread

3 tablespoons fresh flat-leaf parsley, finely chopped

⅓ red (bell) pepper

2 teaspoons each ground cumin and ground coriander

1 teaspoon chilli/hot red pepper flakes

2 tablespoons plain/all-purpose flour

2 teaspoons baking powder

1 litre/quart vegetable oil, for deep frying

taratoor sauce

175 ml/¾ cup tahini

juice of 2 lemons

1 garlic clove, minced

175 ml/¾ cup water

1 teaspoon sea salt

a handful of fresh flat-leaf parsley, finely chopped

to serve

a few leaves cos/Romaine lettuce

8 pitta/pita breads, toasted

2 tomatoes, sliced

a handful of fresh flat-leaf parsley, finely chopped

fresh mint leaves, coarsely chopped

sea salt and freshly ground black pepper

4 gherkins/pickles

serves 4

CLASSIC FALAFEL

EVERYONE NEEDS A BASIC GO-TO FALAFEL RECIPE. ONCE YOU MASTER THE TEXTURE, YOU CAN ALTER THE FLAVOUR TO PERSONAL TASTE BY ADDING DIFFERENT COMBINATIONS AND STRENGTHS OF HERBS, SPICES AND GARLIC TO SUIT.

★ Soak the chickpeas in a large bowl of cold water for at least 12 hours.

★ Drain the chickpeas and add to a food processor, along with the onion, salt, black pepper, garlic, bread, parsley, red (bell) pepper, cumin and ground coriander. Blend until it reaches a granular consistency. Add the flour, 2 teaspoons of baking powder and 175 ml/¾ cup water and mix well.

★ Moisten your hands and form small balls of the chickpea mixture and flatten them slightly.

★ Heat the vegetable oil in a deep-fat fryer or a large frying pan/skillet to 190°C (375°F) or until the oil is bubbling steadily. Fry the chickpea balls until golden brown. Remove the falafel and drain carefully using paper towels.

★ For the taratoor sauce, in a deep bowl, beat the tahini with the lemon juice and minced garlic until it becomes quite creamy. Add the water little by little, and continue to beat well. Add the salt and parsley and stir. Taste and if the sauce isn't tangy enough, add a little bit more lemon juice. Refrigerate until ready to use.

★ To serve, stuff a couple of lettuce leaves into each pitta/pita bread and add 2–3 falafel. Add the tomato slices, parsley, mint and salt and pepper. Drizzle on the sauce and serve with a gherkin/pickle.

CHAPTER 7
SAUCES & SIDES

ELEVATE YOUR MEATBALL DISHES OR FIND THE PERFECT
COMPANION FOR THEM WITH A WIDE RANGE OF TASTY SAUCES
AND ACCOMPANIMENTS. THERE'S SOMETHING FOR EVERYONE,
FROM DAINTY DIPS TO HEARTY SIDES.

GUACAMOLE

6 ripe Hass avocados, halved and stoned/pitted

½ red onion, finely chopped

a handful of freshly chopped coriander/cilantro

2 red chillies/chiles, finely chopped

juice of 2 limes

2–3 pinches of sea salt

Tabasco and cayenne pepper (optional)

makes 700 g/25 oz.

★ Scoop the flesh out of the avocado with a tablespoon into a shallow bowl. Add the onion, coriander/cilantro and chillies/chiles.

★ Add the lime juice, then mash everything together with a fork, leaving the texture quite chunky.

★ Season with salt to taste. Add a few dashes of Tabasco and sprinkle with cayenne pepper, if you like.

BEET HUMMUS

140 g/1 cup canned chickpeas, drained and rinsed
250 g/2 scant cups beetroot/beets, cooked and cubed
1 fat garlic clove
2 tablespoons olive oil
1 tablespoon freshly squeezed lemon juice
2 tablespoons tahini
2–3 pinches sea salt

makes 400 g/14 oz.

★ Put all of the ingredients in a food processor or blender and blitz until smooth. Taste and adjust the seasoning, if necessary.

BLUE CHEESE DIP

150 g/scant ¾ cup Greek/strained plain yogurt

150 ml/scant ¾ cup sour cream

90 g/generous ¾ cup blue cheese, such as Stilton or Gorgonzola

3 tablespoons mayonnaise

a pinch of salt

a splash of Worcestershire sauce or freshly squeezed lemon juice

1 tablespoon snipped chives, plus extra for decoration

makes 400 g/14 oz.

★ Put all of the ingredients except the chives in a food processor or blender, and blitz until smooth.

★ Transfer to a serving bowl and stir in the chives. Sprinkle some extra chives on top for decoration.

TZATZIKI

1 large, firm cucumber

½ teaspoon salt

400 g/2 scant cups Greek/strained plain yogurt

2 tablespoons freshly chopped dill, plus extra to garnish (optional)

2 garlic cloves, crushed

2 pinches salt

1 tablespoon olive oil

makes 500 g/1 lb. 2 oz.

★ Peel, deseed and dice the cucumber. Sprinkle it with the salt, mix well and set aside for 5 minutes.

★ Wrap the cucumber in a clean kitchen cloth and squeeze to remove the liquid from the cucumber.

★ Put the cucumber in a bowl and add the remaining ingredients. Mix together well and serve, garnished with dill, if you like.

ROAST CARROT, GINGER & MISO DIP

300 g/10½ oz. carrots, peeled and thinly sliced

25 g/1 oz. grated fresh ginger

3 tablespoons white miso paste

2 tablespoons tahini

sesame seeds, to garnish (optional)

makes 350 g/12 oz.

★ Preheat the oven to 180°C (350°F) Gas 4.

★ Put the carrots in a roasting pan and roast in the preheated oven for 20–25 minutes until softened. Set aside until cool.

★ Blitz the cooled carrots in a food processor or blender together with the ginger, miso and tahini. Serve, sprinkled with sesame seeds, if desired.

HOMEMADE TOMATO KETCHUP

SO MUCH DEEPER AND RICHER THAN OUT OF A BOTTLE...JUST WAIT AND SEE. PARTICULARLY GOOD WITH BEEF MEATBALLS.

2 tablespoons olive oil
1 onion, finely chopped
2 garlic cloves, crushed
450 ml/2 scant cups passata/strained tomatoes
150 ml/⅔ cup red wine vinegar
150 g/¾ cup soft brown sugar
2 tablespoons black treacle/dark molasses
2 tablespoons tomato purée/paste
1 teaspoon Dijon mustard
2 bay leaves
1 teaspoon sea salt
½ teaspoon freshly ground black pepper

makes about 400 ml/1¾ cups

★ Heat the oil in a saucepan, add the onion and garlic and fry gently for 10 minutes until softened. Add all the remaining ingredients, bring to the boil, reduce the heat and simmer gently for 30 minutes until thickened and reduced by about one third.

★ Pass the sauce through a sieve/strainer, let cool and pour into a clean bottle and store in the fridge for up to five days. If using sterilized bottles, pour the hot sauce directly into the bottle and when cold, seal and store in the fridge. It will keep for a few weeks.

FRESH AÏOLI

THIS IS AN ALL-TIME CLASSIC SPANISH DIP, PARTICULARLY BRILLIANT WITH FISH, PRAWNS/SHRIMP OR CHICKEN. THIS RECIPE HAS A WONDERFUL ROBUST GARLICKY FLAVOUR.

2 large egg yolks
4 very fresh garlic cloves, crushed
1 teaspoon Dijon mustard
150 ml/⅔ cup good-quality light olive oil
freshly squeezed juice of ½ lemon
sea salt and freshly ground black pepper

makes about 200 ml/¾ cup

★ Beat the eggs yolks in a large bowl with a balloon whisk. Add the garlic and mustard and beat through. While beating the mixture, slowly add the olive oil in a thin, steady stream. When all the oil has been added, the aïoli should have a smooth, velvety appearance. Add the lemon juice, season with salt and pepper and gently stir through.
Refrigerate until needed.

SWEET CHILLI/CHILE SAUCE

SWEET CHILLI/CHILE SAUCE GOES WITH ALMOST ANYTHING, FROM SALADS AND VEGETABLES TO BEEF AND CHICKEN. YOU NAME IT, IT TASTES GREAT WITH IT!

6 large red chillies/chiles, deseeded and chopped
4 garlic cloves, chopped
1 teaspoon grated/minced root ginger
1 teaspoon salt
100 ml/⅓ cup rice wine vinegar
100 g/½ cup castor/superfine sugar

makes about 200 ml/generous ¾ cup

★ Put the chillies/chiles, garlic, ginger and salt in a food processor and blend to a coarse paste. Transfer to a saucepan, add the vinegar and sugar, bring to the boil and simmer gently, part-covered, for 5 minutes until the mixture becomes a thin syrup. Remove from the heat and let cool.

★ Pour into an airtight container and store in the fridge for up to 2 weeks.

ASIAN BARBECUE SAUCE

FOR SOMETHING A LITTLE DIFFERENT ON THE SIDE, GIVE THIS FRAGRANT BARBECUE SAUCE A TRY. YOU COULD ALSO USE IT TO MARINADE MEATBALLS BEFORE COOKING. LOVELY WITH PORK BALLS.

100 ml/⅓ cup passata/strained tomatoes
50 ml/3½ tablespoons hoisin sauce
1 teaspoon hot chilli/chile sauce
2 garlic cloves, crushed
2 tablespoons sweet soy sauce
1 tablespoon rice wine vinegar
1 teaspoon ground coriander
½ teaspoon ground cinnamon
¼ teaspoon Chinese five-spice powder

makes about 350 ml/1½ cups

★ Put all the ingredients into a small saucepan, add 100 ml/⅓ cup water, bring to the boil and simmer gently for 10 minutes. Remove the saucepan from the heat and let cool.

★ Pour into an airtight container and store in the fridge for up to 2 weeks.

PROPER GRAVY

THIS IS A THICKENED BEEF GRAVY WHICH SHOULD LIGHTLY COAT MEAT AND VEGETABLES. SERVE WITH BALLS AND MASHED POTATOES.

1 tablespoon fat from a pan used to cook beef in

1 onion, thinly sliced

250 ml/1 cup good beef stock

2 teaspoons cornflour/cornstarch, mixed with 2 teaspoons cold water

sea salt and freshly ground black pepper

serves 4–6

★ In a saucepan, heat the fat, add the onion and cook slowly over a low heat until browned, about 30 minutes. Do not let it burn.

★ Add the stock and cornflour/cornstarch mixture, then season to taste. Stir constantly over a low heat until the mixture boils and simmer for a couple of minutes. Strain if you wish or serve as it is.

BÉCHAMEL SAUCE

A CREAMY CHEESE SAUCE THAT CAN BE USED AS A BASE FOR MEATBALL AND PASTA DISHES. COMBINING CHEDDAR AND MONTEREY JACK GIVES THIS SAUCE A DELICIOUS DEPTH OF FLAVOUR.

50 g/3½ tablespoons unsalted butter

60 g/6 tablespoons plain/all-purpose flour

625 ml/2½ cups whole milk

1 teaspoon fine sea salt

150 g/1¼ cups grated Monterey Jack or other mild, semi-hard cheese

150 g/1¼ cups grated medium Cheddar cheese

serves 6–8

★ Melt the butter in a saucepan. Stir in the flour and cook, stirring constantly, for 1 minute. Pour in the milk in a steady stream, whisking constantly, and continue to whisk for 3–5 minutes until the sauce begins to thicken. Season with fine sea salt. Remove from the heat and add the cheeses, mixing well with a spoon to incorporate. Taste and adjust the seasoning.

APPLE SAUCE

INFUSED WITH APPLE AND LEMONY ZINGINESS, THIS IS IDEAL FOR ADDING ANOTHER DIMENSION TO PORK MEATBALLS.

2 teaspoons butter
5–6 cooking apples, peeled, cored and diced
finely grated zest of ½ lemon
juice of 1 lemon
a pinch of ground cinnamon
1 tablespoon soft light brown sugar
100 ml/scant ½ cup water
salt, to taste

serves 4–6

★ Melt the butter in a saucepan over a medium heat. Add all the other ingredients and bring to the boil, then reduce the heat to a low simmer and leave for 20–30 minutes until thick and the apples are soft, stirring occasionally to make sure it's not catching on the base of the pan. Add salt to taste.

★ Either mash it with a potato masher or purée it in a food processor, or just dish it up chunky, depending on your preference.

★ Store in the fridge for up to 2 weeks in a sealed container.

CRANBERRY SAUCE

FEATURING CINNAMON AND LEMON, THIS CRANBERRY SAUCE IS PERFECT FOR PAIRING WITH BALLS FROM THE POULTRY CHAPTER.

1½ tablespoons butter
1 red onion, finely chopped
2 handfuls of fresh cranberries (frozen cranberries, defrosted, work well here, as well)
a big pinch of cinnamon
2 tablespoons white wine vinegar
1 tablespoon soft dark brown sugar
juice of ½ lemon

serves 4–6

★ In a frying pan/skillet, heat the butter over a medium heat and fry the onion until soft and golden brown.

★ Add the cranberries and cinnamon, then fry for 1 minute. Pour in the white wine vinegar and bring to the boil, then sprinkle in the sugar and keep mixing well. Add the lemon juice, stir and remove from the heat. Serve immediately while hot or chill and serve as a cold accompaniment.

★ Store in the fridge for up to 2 weeks in a sealed container.

FANCY MASHED POTATOES

WHEN UNINSPIRING MASH JUST ISN'T GOING TO DO IT FOR YOU, THIS IS A CREAMY, CHEESY GODSEND.

3–4 potatoes, peeled and quartered
1½ tablespoons butter
40 g/½ cup finely grated Parmesan cheese (optional)
2 tablespoons double/heavy cream
sea salt and freshly ground black pepper

serves 4

★ Bring a saucepan of salted water to the boil, add the potatoes and cook for 25 minutes until totally soft when you prod them with a fork.

★ Drain and return to the pan. Add the butter and mash until lovely and soft. Mix in the Parmesan cheese, if using, and then the double/heavy cream, salt and pepper.

★ Serve immediately or use within in 2 days (keep sealed in the fridge and make sure you cool it fully before moving it to the fridge so that it doesn't sweat).

CELERIAC GRATIN

----

2 tablespoons butter
3–4 shallots, finely chopped
1 leek, finely chopped
2 garlic cloves, crushed
1 teaspoon ground Ancho or other dried chilli
a few wild garlic or spinach leaves, roughly chopped
150 ml/⅔ cup whole milk
100 ml/scant ½ cup double/heavy cream
1 green chilli/chile, deseeded and finely chopped
600 g/1 lb. 4 oz. potatoes, thinly sliced
150 g/5 oz. celeriac/celery root, peeled and thinly sliced
50 g/½ cup grated Parmesan
olive oil, for drizzling
sea salt and freshly ground black pepper

serves 4

★ Preheat the oven to 180°C (350°F) Gas 4.

★ Melt the butter in a frying pan/skillet and gently fry the shallots, leek and garlic with the ground Ancho for about 10 minutes, or until soft. Add the wild garlic leaves or spinach and allow to wilt over gentle heat.

★ In a separate pan, heat the milk, cream and chilli/chile over a low heat for about 10 minutes to infuse the milk with the chilli/chile flavour.

★ Put the potato and celeriac/celery root slices into a large bowl. Add the cooked leek mixture and mix well, ensuring everything is evenly coated. Layer the slices in a greased ovenproof dish, seasoning well between each layer. Pour the infused milk mixture over the vegetables, ensuring that the shredded chilli is evenly distributed. Sprinkle the Parmesan over the top and season with a little extra salt and pepper. Cover the dish with foil and bake in the preheated oven for about 1 hour. Remove the foil and drizzle olive oil evenly over the gratin. Put back in the oven, uncovered, and cook for about 15 minutes, or until the potatoes are nicely golden.

PATATAS BRAVAS

KNOWN WORLDWIDE AS A GREAT TAPAS DISH, THIS CLASSIC SPANISH RECIPE TAKES ALL THE FLAVOURS OF RURAL SPAIN AND COMBINES THEM TO WONDERFUL EFFECT. SERVE WITH ALBONDIGAS, AÏOLI AND SALT COD FRITTERS AS PART OF A DELICIOUS TAPAS FEAST.

400 g/14 oz. new waxy potatoes

1 tablespoon olive oil

2 garlic cloves, crushed

1 hot red chilli/chile, deseeded and finely chopped

2–3 large, ripe tomatoes, roughly chopped

a pinch of sweet smoked paprika (pimentón dulce)

½ teaspoon paprika

a pinch of saffron strands

1 teaspoon dried wild oregano

2 tablespoons olive oil (or 1 tablespoon olive oil and 1 tablespoon chilli oil)

sea salt flakes and freshly ground black pepper

serves 4

★ Cut the potatoes into 2-cm/¾-inch pieces. Put them in a large saucepan of lightly salted boiling water, cover and bring back to the boil. Cook until they are cooked through but still firm. Drain and pat dry with paper towels.

★ Put the 1 tablespoon oil in a small frying pan/skillet over a medium heat and fry the garlic and chilli/chile for about 1 minute. Add the tomatoes and cook for a further 2 minutes. Add both types of paprika, the saffron and oregano. Stir and cook for a further 5–10 minutes until the flavours have fully mingled and the tomatoes have softened. Remove from the heat and cover.

★ Put the 2 tablespoons oil in a large frying pan/skillet over a medium–high heat and fry the dry cubes of potato until golden brown and crispy. Season these with salt and pepper and serve topped with the spicy tomato sauce.

THE ULTIMATE ARRABBIATA SAUCE

ARRABBIATA LITERALLY MEANS 'ANGRY', REFERRING TO THE HEAT OF THE CHILLI/CHILE PEPPERS. WHEN IT'S DONE WELL, WITH RIPE TOMATOES AND FRESH RED CHILLI/CHILE, IT IS TRULY HEAVENLY.

500 g/1 lb. 2 oz. ripe plum tomatoes

4 tablespoons olive oil

2 garlic cloves, bruised and skin on

2 tablespoons Italian red wine

1 red chilli/chile, cut lengthways and deseeded

fresh rosemary sprig

1 fresh bay leaf

½ teaspoon dried oregano

8–10 fresh basil leaves, torn, plus extra to serve

sea salt and freshly ground black pepper

penne or spaghetti, to serve

grated Parmesan cheese, to serve

serves 2

★ To skin the tomatoes, place them in a small bowl and pour enough boiling water over them to cover. Leave for a few seconds until the tomato skins split, then drain the water, run under cold water until the tomatoes are cool enough to handle and peel off the skins. Quarter the tomatoes and remove the seeds.

★ Heat the oil in a saucepan over medium heat and fry the garlic cloves for a few seconds, then add the wine. Allow to simmer for 30 seconds, then add the chopped tomatoes. Add the chilli/chile, rosemary, bay leaf, dried oregano and ½ teaspoon salt, stir and turn the heat down to low so that the sauce is just gently simmering. Cover with a lid and gently cook for about 40–45 minutes.

★ While the sauce is cooking, give it an occasional stir and taste to check the heat level of the sauce. Once the required level is reached, you can remove and discard the chilli/chile. Add a splash of water if the sauce is becoming too dry in the pan. Once cooked, stir through the basil leaves.

★ This sauce is a perfect accompaniment to penne or spaghetti. To serve, toss some cooked pasta in the sauce, making sure it is nicely coated. Serve dressed with a little more olive oil, a good grating of Parmesan, some black pepper and a few more fresh basil leaves.

Note: It is crucial to use ripe tomatoes for this recipe. If these are not available, use canned chopped tomatoes, but drain the juice and simmer for an additional 20–30 minutes.

THE PERFECT PUTTANESCA SAUCE

THE FLAVOURS OF THIS PUTTANESCA CAPTURE THE SUNSHINE OF SOUTHERN ITALY PERFECTLY. IT IS ROBUST, SALTY AND SATISFYING; QUICK TO MAKE, BUT WITH WONDERFULLY WELL-BALANCED FLAVOURS. BE SURE TO EAT IT STRAIGHT AWAY.

50 g/1¾ oz. anchovy fillets in brine or olive oil, drained

3 tablespoons extra virgin olive oil

2 garlic cloves, thinly sliced

1 small, hot, red chilli/chile, deseeded and finely chopped

500 g/1 lb. 2 oz. ripe plum tomatoes, skinned

50 g/⅓ cup capers

40 g/¼ cup green olives, stoned/pitted and chopped

2 tablespoons tomato purée/paste

100 g/⅔ cup black or Kalamata olives, stoned/pitted and chopped

sea salt and freshly ground black pepper

serves 2

★ Rinse the anchovy fillets under cold water for a few moments to desalt or remove excess oil. Pat the fillets dry on some paper towels. Chop roughly.

★ Heat the oil in a saucepan and fry the garlic and chilli/chile for about 3–4 minutes. Keep it moving but allow a little browning. Add the anchovies and continue to fry for about 1 minute, or until they begin to break down. Add the chopped tomatoes, capers, green olives and tomato purée/paste. Stir thoroughly. Turn the heat down and allow to gently bubble away, uncovered, for 20 minutes.

★ Add the black olives and cook for a further 5 minutes. Season only at the end of cooking, as there is already quite a hit of salt from the anchovies and the capers.

★ Make sure you serve it straight away!

JEWELLED RICE

600 ml/2½ cups water

sea salt

a pinch of saffron fronds/threads

450 g/2¼ cups basmati long-grain rice, rinsed and drained

2 tablespoons barberries

2 tablespoons dried sour/tart cherries or cranberries

2 tablespoons currants

2 tablespoons golden sultanas

2 tablespoons raisins

2 tablespoons caster/granulated sugar

2 tablespoons orange blossom water

2 tablespoons freshly squeezed lemon juice

2 tablespoons bitter orange rind, very finely sliced

2 tablespoons olive oil with a knob/pat of butter

120 g/1 cup blanched almonds, cut into slivers

120 g/1 cup unsalted pistachio kernels, cut into slivers

2 tablespoons pine nuts

2 tablespoons dried apricots, finely sliced

icing/confectioners' sugar and rose petals, to serve

serves 6

THIS IS A TRULY SUMPTUOUS RICE DISH, AS BEAUTIFUL TO BEHOLD AS IT IS TO TASTE, WITH ITS COLOURFUL DRIED FRUIT, NUTS AND FRAGRANT ROSE PETALS. PERFECT SERVED WITH A MEATBALL TAGINE.

★ Pour the water into a pot and bring it to the boil with a pinch of salt. Stir in the saffron fronds/threads and the rice and continue to boil for 3–4 minutes, then reduce the heat and simmer for 10 minutes until the water has been absorbed. Turn off the heat, cover the pot with a clean kitchen cloth, put on the lid and leave the rice to steam a further 10 minutes. Meanwhile, put the barberries, sour/tart cherries, currants, sultanas and raisins into a bowl. Pour over enough boiling water to cover them, and soak for 5 minutes, then drain and put aside.

★ In a small pot, stir the sugar with the orange blossom water and lemon juice until the sugar has dissolved. Bring the liquid to the boil, stir in the orange rind and simmer for 5 minutes. Turn off the heat and put aside.

★ In a wide, heavy-based pan, heat up the olive oil and butter and stir in the nuts and apricots for 1–2 minutes, until they emit a lovely aroma. Toss in the soaked dried fruits for 1–2 minutes, until they plump up. Tip the rice into the pan and mix thoroughly. Lift the orange rind out of the syrup and toss most of it through the rice. Tip the rice in a mound on a serving dish. Scatter the rest of the orange rind over the top and drizzle the syrup on top. Dust with icing/confectioners' sugar and rose petals.

GRILLED AUBERGINE/ EGGPLANT & BELL PEPPER SALAD

AUBERGINES/EGGPLANTS PLAY A HUGE ROLE ON THE MEZZE TABLE –
THERE ARE REPUTED TO BE AROUND 200 DISHES MADE WITH THEM –
AND SMOKING THEM OVER A GAS FLAME, OR ON A CHARCOAL GRILL, IS
ONE OF THE MOST ENJOYABLE WAYS OF COOKING AND EATING THEM.

2–3 large aubergines/eggplants

2 red (bell) peppers

2–3 garlic cloves, crushed

3–4 spring onions/scallions, trimmed and finely sliced

a bunch of fresh flat-leaf parsley, coarsely chopped

sea salt and freshly ground black pepper

2–3 tablespoons olive oil

2 tablespoons pomegranate syrup/molasses, or the freshly squeezed juice of 1 lemon, plus extra for drizzling

serves 4–6

★ Put the aubergines/eggplants and (bell) peppers directly on the gas flame, or on the grid over a charcoal grill. Over the flame, the skins of the aubergines/eggplants and peppers will buckle and flake a little and will make a bit of a mess of your gas cooker but, over the charcoal grill, the skins will toughen and brown, leaving no mess! It doesn't matter which method you choose, but you are looking for the flesh of both the aubergines/eggplants and the peppers to soften, so you need to keep turning them to make sure they are evenly smoked. Once soft, pop them both into a clean, resealable plastic bag to sweat for 5 minutes, then hold them by the stalks under cold running water and peel off the skins. Squeeze out the excess water and put them on a chopping board. Remove the stalks of the aubergines/eggplants and chop the flesh to a coarse pulp. Remove the stalks and seeds of the peppers and chop the flesh to a coarse pulp as well.

★ Tip the pulped flesh into a bowl and add the garlic, spring onions/ scallions and parsley. Season well with salt and pepper (the smoked aubergine/eggplant needs salt to bring out the flavour) and bind the salad with the olive oil and pomegranate syrup/molasses or lemon juice. Drizzle a little extra pomegranate syrup/molasses over the top before serving.

STIR-FRIED NOODLES & BEANSPROUTS

200 g/7 oz. glass noodles

a dash of cooking oil

2 Asian shallots, finely chopped

3 tablespoons light soy sauce

a pinch of black pepper

a pinch of pork or vegetable bouillon (optional)

1 bird's eye chilli/chile, thinly sliced

100 ml/⅓ cup white wine or water

160 g/2¾ cups beansprouts

a handful of garlic chives, cut into 2-cm/¾-inch lengths (optional), or garden mint

2 sprigs of coriander/cilantro, chopped

2 big tablespoons roasted salted peanuts, crushed

dipping sauce (optional)

1 bird's eye chilli/chile, sliced

3 tablespoons soy sauce

serves 2

THIS SOUTHEAST ASIAN DISH FEATURES A LOVELY BALANCE OF FLAVOURS. THE PEANUTS ADD TEXTURE AND CONTRAST WITH THE VERY SILKY GLASS NOODLES, AND EACH AND EVERY SIMPLE AND MODEST INGREDIENT STANDS OUT. THE DIPPING SAUCE PROVIDES AN EXTRA SALTY, SPICY KICK. SERVE TOPPED WITH ANY OF THE ASIAN-INSPIRED MEATBALLS IN THIS BOOK.

★ Put the noodles in a bowl, cover with warm water and allow to soak for 30 minutes. After 30 minutes, cut them into shorter lengths.

★ Heat the oil in a frying pan over low–medium heat and fry the shallots for about 5 minutes. Add the noodles, soy sauce, pepper and bouillon, if using, and stir-fry for 2–3 minutes.

★ Add the chilli/chile, wine and beansprouts. Stir-fry for 2 minutes, then remove from the heat and mix in the garlic chives, coriander/cilantro and peanuts. Serve hot or at room temperature.

★ To make the dipping sauce, simply crush the chilli/chile into the soy sauce with the back of a spoon.

PENANG HOT-AND-SOUR NOODLE SOUP

BEEF, PORK OR CHICKEN MEATBALLS WOULD ALL WORK WELL IN THIS SPICY SOUP. IF YOU CAN'T GET HOLD OF THE MUCH UNDERRATED LOTUS ROOT, SUBSTITUTE WITH SLICED WATER CHESTNUTS INSTEAD.

6 red chillies/chiles, stems removed

2 small red onions, unpeeled and halved

2 lemongrass stalks

1 tablespoon paprika

vegetable oil, if needed

1 litre/quart vegetable stock

3 tablespoons vegan fish sauce, or light soy sauce with a pinch of seaweed flakes

2 tablespoons tamarind pulp, or 2 teaspoons tamarind concentrate/paste

1–2 teaspoons salt, to taste

1–2 tablespoons soft brown sugar, or rice syrup, to taste

375 g/13 oz. thick round rice noodles or egg-free yellow noodles

fresh toppings

½ cucumber, halved lengthways

1 fresh lotus root, peeled

a handful of Vietnamese mint leaves, or a mixture of mint and basil leaves

a handful of laksa leaves

1 small red onion, thinly sliced

1 bird's eye chilli/chile, finely chopped

serves 4–6

★ Preheat the oven to 200°C (400°F) Gas 6.

★ Put the chillies/chiles and onions on a baking sheet and roast for 10–15 minutes until starting to blacken at the edges. Let cool, then peel the onions.

★ Put the lemongrass in a food processor and add the paprika, roasted chillies/chiles and onions, then blend to a paste, adding a little oil if needed to thin the mixture. Put the paste in a wok or large frying pan/skillet over a high heat and cook for 2 minutes. Add the stock, 1 litre/quart water, the vegan fish sauce and tamarind to the pan. Bring to the boil over a high heat and simmer briskly for 8–10 minutes. Add salt and sugar to taste. Meanwhile, soak the noodles in hot water for 10 minutes, then drain in a colander.

★ To prepare the fresh toppings, using a teaspoon, scrape out the watery seeds from the centre of the cucumber. Thinly slice the cucumber and lotus root. Blanch the sliced lotus root in boiling water for 1 minute, then set aside.

★ Divide the noodles among serving bowls, then add a selection of the fresh toppings. Ladle over the broth to ensure the noodles are well covered. Serve.

INDEX

RECIPE CREDITS

Annie Rigg
Spanish albondigas

Belinda Williams
Meatball, lentil & curly kale soup

Brian Glover
Pork & courgette/zucchini meatballs

Brontë Aurell
Swedish meatballs

Carol Hilker
Classic falafel
Classic spaghetti & meatballs
Sweet & sour chicken balls

Cathy Seward
Bitterballen
Buffalo chicken balls
Chinese Lionhead meatballs
Chinese shrimp balls
Christmas turkey meatballs
Crispy duck bonbons
Cuban Papas Rellenas
Faggots
Giant lamb & mint balls
Japanese Tsukune chicken meatballs
Königsberger Klopse
Malai kofta with fruit & nut filling
Smoked mackerel, potato & dill balls
Sweet potato, kale & quinoa balls
Thai salmon balls

Chloe Coker & Jane Montgomery
Lemon & mushroom risotto balls
Winter vegetable stew with herbed
    dumplings

Clare Ferguson
Italian swordfish balls
Jewish mother's chicken soup

Dan May
Celeriac gratin
Fresh aioli
Patatas bravas
The perfect puttanesca pasta sauce
The ultimate arrabbiata pasta sauce

Dunja Gulin
'Raw' falafel

Ghillie Başan
Arancini with pecorino, porcini &
    mozzarella
Asian pork kofta

Chilli beef tartare & bulgur balls
Grilled aubergine/eggplant & bell
    pepper salad
Jewelled rice
Kefta tagine with eggs & cumin
Kefta tagine with lemon
Meatballs in an egg & lemon sauce
Mini fish kefta with saffron & lemon
Mini meatballs stuffed with roasted
    pistachios
Mother-in-law's meatballs
Spicy bean balls
Tagine of spicy kefta with lemon
Turmeric fish balls with sunflower
    seeds

Jackie Kearney
Doodhi bottle gourd kofta masala
Penang hot-and-sour noodle soup
Popcorn tofu balls

Jenny Linford
Garlic chive meatballs
Ricotta & spinach dumplings with
    cherry tomato sauce
Spicy Indian garlic meatballs

Jordan Bourke
Crab cake balls
Spicy Spanish meatballs

Julz Beresford
Spanish cheese balls
Salt cod albondigas

Laura Washburn
Béchamel sauce
Chicken meatballs with roasted
    vegetables
Macaroni meatball bake
Meatball & fontina sandwich
Meatball tagine
Meatballs in red pepper sauce
Nutty meatballs
Ragù arancini

Linda Collister
Thai meatballs with chicken

Liz Franklin
Cheddar cheese & tuna fish balls

Louise Pickford
Asian barbecue sauce
Sweet chilli/chile sauce
Vietnamese pork ball skewers

Lydia France
Mini pork balls with cider syrup

Maxine Clark
Pancetta & fennel puffs
Pork & fennel meatballs

Milli Taylor
Beetroot hummus
Blue cheese dip
Guacamole
Roast carrot, ginger & miso dip
Tzatziki

Miranda Ballard
Apple sauce
Cranberry sauce
Homemade ketchup
Fancy mashed potatoes
Wurst meatballs

Rachael Anne Hill
Goulash meatballs
Mini meatballs with five-veg sauce

Rena Salaman
Lebanese meatballs with pine nuts

Ross Dobson
Easy sausage meatballs with garlic
    bread
Moroccan meatball stew
Naked spinach & ricotta ravioli
Salt cod, potato & butter bean fritters

Silvana Franco
Pancetta & chicken meatballs

Sonia Stevenson
Proper gravy

Sunil Vijayakar
Curried lamb balls

Tonia George
Italian polpette

Tori Haschka
Deep-dish meatball pizza pie
Greek lamb balls with fava
Tomato Keftedes

Tori Finch
Scotch quails' eggs

Uyen Luu
Stir-fried noodles & beansprouts

Valerie Aikman-Smith
Olive suppli

Vatcharin Bhumichitr
Yellow bean balls

Vicky Jones
Brazilian black-eyed bean & shrimp
    fritters

Ryland Peters & Small
Frikadelle
Thai pork & rice soup

PICTURE CREDITS

Jan Baldwin 2, 32, 59, 69, 89, 139;
Steve Baxter 10, 113; Martin
Brigdale 15, 51, 64, 76, 91, 132; Peter
Cassidy 8, 13, 33, 53, 65, 78, 83, 86,
90, 102, 111, 121, 126, 130, 135-137;
Helen Cathcart 128, 129; Jean
Cazals 40; Vanessa Davies 82; Tara
Fisher 26, 97; Georgia Glynn-Smith
55; Jonathan Gregson 114; Richard
Jung 45, 54; Lisa Linder 98; William
Lingwood 44, 77; Jason Lowe 34;
David Munns 21; Steve Painter 6,
16, 19, 25, 27, 31, 39, 47, 56, 60, 70,
72, 75, 81, 84, 92, 95, 101, 107, 108,
124, 138; William Reavell 11, 48, 96,
112, 116; Yuki Sugiura 36; Ian
Wallace 41, 131, 133; Kate Whitaker
20, 22, 66, 71, 104, 110, 115; Isobel
Wield 28, 63, 120; Clare Winfield
14, 42, 117, 119, 122, 140, 141